PRISON W

THE ROAD MAP TO NEGOTIATIONS

The Road Map to Negotiations
Abdullah Öcalan
Original title:
"Türkiye'de demokratikleşme sorunları, Kürdistan'da çözüm modelleri (Yol haritası)",
translated in English to be
"Problems of Democratization in Turkey and Solution Models in Kurdistan (Road Map)"

Published by
International Initiative Edition
International Initiative
"Freedom for Abdullah Öcalan—Peace in Kurdistan"
P.O. Box 100 511
D-50445 Cologne
www.freedom-for-ocalan.com

and

Mesopotamien Verlags- und Vertriebs GmbH
Gladbacher Str. 407 B
D-41460 Neuss
www.pirtuk.info

Translation: Havin Guneser
Typesetting and cover design: Holger Deilke

Cover motive: Şewqa evînê welat II (Dawn of Love for Homeland II, detail) by Rodi Khalil
70 x 50 cm, mixed technique, natural color with pigment

ISBN 978-3-941012-43-1

first edition February 2012

CONTENTS

The Road to the Road Map

Editorial Notes by the International Initiative

The "Road Map" is an extraordinary document. It was the centerpiece of the secret dialogue process between Abdullah Öcalan and the Turkish state that started in 2009 and was broken off in mid-2011. This was not the first time the state approached Öcalan for talks—it had been making other efforts since the early 1990s, before and after his abduction. But these later talks were by far the most serious of all.

In early 2009 the state delegation, led by Hakan Fidan, the present director of the national intelligence service MİT, approached Öcalan, undoubtedly the most influential Kurdish politician in Turkey, and requested that he produce a comprehensive statement of his views. Öcalan announced publicly that he would write such a road map and at the same time called on intellectuals, journalists, comrades and friends of the Kurdish people around the world to submit their opinions on a road map to the democratization of Turkey and a solution to the Kurdish question.

In so doing, he was also trying to break the isolation he has been held under ever since his abduction on February 15, 1999. He has no means of communication to discuss opinions with people outside prison. He cannot write or receive letters; he cannot make phone calls or receive visits from anyone except his siblings or lawyers. For almost eleven years he has been the sole prisoner on İmralı Island, locked in his cell for twenty-three hours per day and guarded by one thousand soldiers, stationed in this newly declared military area. These conditions have rightfully earned the İmralı Island prison the nickname "the European Guantánamo."

At the time a change seemed possible, since the Turkish government seemed to be making a serious effort to solve Turkey's most vital problem, the Kurdish issue. Experts were asked for their opinions; reports were solicited from academics. Prime Minister Erdoğan declared the issue "his personal problem." President Abdullah Gül promised that "good things are about to happen." The government announced the "Kurdish opening." The PKK upheld a unilateral ceasefire. Hopes ran high that the mistakes of the past would finally be rectified.

Öcalan's call for opinions was discussed widely in the press and created a lot of publicity for this Road Map even before it was written. At the same time it highlighted the fact that the government was not presenting its own comprehensive plan. As a well-known Turkish journalist, close to the military, put it: "We know the outlines of Öcalan's plan—but where is Erdoğan's plan?"

Öcalan finished writing this text on August 15, 2009, exactly twenty-five years after the beginning of the armed struggle, and addressed it to the European Court of Human Rights in Strasbourg, France, as part of a complaint, pending since 2003, about his isolation conditions. But in an unprecedented move, the Turkish government prevented the document from being delivered to the court for eighteen months, despite repeated requests from Strasbourg. It was a bad omen.

Shortly afterward, in October 2009, at Öcalan's behest and in accordance with state authorities, a "peace delegation" of twenty-six unarmed guerrilla fighters and political refugees entered Turkey from Iraq at the Habur border gate. After a brief detention, they were released—at which point tens of thousands of jubilant Kurds, feeling that peace was finally close at hand, welcomed them frenetically. But the government had not announced a peace delegation's arrival in advance—but called it a "surrender"; and Turkish nationalists expressed outrage at the Kurdish display of joy. Erdoğan might have shown some courage and declared that the joy was natural since the bloodshed was about to end—had he done so, things might have taken a different course. But from then on the "Kurdish opening" faltered.

In the local elections in April 2009, the pro-Kurdish party had achieved some success. Thereafter the government began to arrest Kurdish politicians and political activists on a mass scale. The arrests have continued, year by year, up to the present (January 2012). More than five thousand people, mostly Kurds, have been arrested in this so-called "KCK operation"; most of them are still in prison, awaiting trial. This operation destroyed all confidence in the "Kurdish opening," a term that by then had fallen into disuse.

When this Road Map finally reached the Court in January 2011, some hope still remained that an agreement might be reached. The state delegation assured Öcalan that Prime Minister Erdoğan agreed with "95 percent of the Road Map." A forty-minute record of one of the parallel talks with senior PKK members confirming this was later leaked to the internet.

Öcalan meanwhile pushed for concrete steps. Again at the government's request, he drew up three short "protocols" on the establishment of a Truth and Reconciliation Commission; the creation of a committee to draw up a democratic constitution; and last but not least, concrete procedures for the PKK's withdrawal and subsequent disarmament. The state delegation placed these protocols in front of senior PKK bodies, who also signed them. Until short before the June 2011 parliamentary elections the delegation promised that the government would respond—positively, it was understood. But no written or verbal response ever arrived at İmralı. The delegation was never seen again. In July 2011, Öcalan stated that under these conditions he had to withdraw from the talks.

The parliamentary elections resulted in a third term for the Erdoğan-led AKP government—whereupon the response finally came, in the form of massive military operations inside and outside Turkey. Chemical weapons have likely been used. In air raids, more than forty civilians have lost their lives—thirty-six alone in one incident in December 2011 near the village Roboskî in Uludere, Şirnak. New waves of mass arrests targeted the political opposition, especially members and supporters of the pro-Kurdish party BDP. By now, the arrest waves were hitting journalists, writers, and academics, leading to ever-louder outcries by human rights organizations and the international press.

Perhaps the most telling response is what happened to Öcalan himself and his legal team. Since July 27, 2011, none of his lawyers have been allowed to visit him. The İmralı Island prison, the "European Guantánamo," is once again in complete isolation. Even worse, on November 22, 2011, in a move unprecedented in the history of Turkey, thirty-six of Öcalan's lawyers were arrested. They are currently in prison awaiting trial. Öcalan has thus been entirely stripped of his right to defense. Furthermore, as this is being written, Öcalan has been completely cut off from the outside world for almost seven months. Strictly speaking, no one even knows if he is still alive.

The AKP government has so totally reversed its approach to the Kurdish issue that one cannot help but wonder how serious the "Kurdish opening" was in the first place. The government and judiciary's furious attacks on Kurds since the summer of 2011, the aggressive military operations, the likely use of chemical weapons, the bombing of civilians, and Öcalan's renewed total isolation have left the Kurds with little hope for a peaceful solution. In many aspects, the situation is worse today than it was in the 1990s.

The difference between the AKP and past governments is that the others did not say they would resolve the Kurdish question while they killed Kurds. But every day the AKP government still speaks of the necessity of resolving the question—yet escalates its use of violence, even committing atrocities, against the Kurdish people, as well as deploying diplomacy. But history has shown repeatedly that no victory can be won in this manner.

This approach, moreover, carries the very real risk that Islamo-nationalism will become an intrinsic part of Turkish society. In the face of such a development, the Kurdish people would find it hard to maintain their belief in and hopes for a common life in Turkey.

Amid all this turmoil, as you will see as you read this book, Öcalan embodies the voice of reason. Before all communication with him was cut in July 2011, he emphasized that for him this Road Map is still valid. Voices from the democratic opposition and even circles close to the government give us confidence that the Road Map retains its influence on both sides. To this day, it is the only nonmilitary solution that has been proposed by anyone.

Developments could still go either way. We still hope that both parties will meet around a table for a peaceful resolution of the Kurdish conflict, for which we have been striving since 1999. We call on everyone to do the same: to work for a peaceful, negotiated solution. In any such future negotiations, the Road Map is very likely to be on the table.

We are happy to publish the English translation of the Road Map and confident that it delivers what the original title promises: "The Problems of Democratization in Turkey and Solution Models in Kurdistan."

International Initiative
"Freedom for Abdullah Öcalan—Peace in Kurdistan"
Cologne, January 2012

Preface to *The Road Map*

By Immanuel Wallerstein

The Road Map offers "a solution to the Kurdish question" in Turkey. But it raises issues that are far more general and widespread than the specific geohistorical questions it discusses. There are, it seems to me, four separate, if deeply intertwined, contradictions within the operations of the modern world-system, which is a capitalist world-economy.

They are:

(1) the search for sovereignty by the states;
(2) the thrust of all states to become nations;
(3) the demands that states be democratic;
(4) the ways that capitalism maintains its equilibrium.

Each of these contradictions requires a book-length exposition to be treated adequately. Here, I can only briefly outline the issues.

(1) Sovereignty: The formal structure of the interstate system that has been created as part of the modern world-system is that all the states are sovereign. Sovereignty in theory means that the states make their decisions autonomously, without interference either from other states or from institutional structures within the boundaries of the state.

Of course, as soon as one asserts these theoretical characteristics, it is obvious that there is not a single state that meets these criteria of sovereignty. It turns out that the claim of a state to be sovereign is just that—a claim, an aspiration, one that some states meet better than others but none meet totally.

Furthermore, notice that it is a claim in two directions—outward beyond the boundaries of a state and inward towards groups within the state. The less a state is able to defend itself outward the more emphasis it places on defending itself against inward erosion of its claim to sovereignty. Republican Turkey falls into this latter category, although of course not only republican Turkey. This is the situation of the vast majority of states in the modern world-system.

(2) **A nation-state:** The basic mechanism by which states seek to defend their sovereignty against groups or institutions within its boundaries is what we have come to call Jacobinism. One can define Jacobinism very simply. It is two things. First, it is the demand that all "citizens" of a state recognize their membership in a single "nation"—however this nation is defined. Secondly, it is the demand that loyalty to this "nation" take priority over all other loyalties of the citizen—loyalties to class, to gender, to a religious group, to an "ethnicity," to kinship groups, in short to any group other than the "nation" as defined by the state.

While the pressure to create this national loyalty (which can then get the label of patriotism) seems to strengthen the state in its outward assertion of sovereignty, it obviously creates significant internal strains. All kinds of groups resist being subordinated to the demand for national loyalty. And sometimes, even often, the resistance becomes violent.

In the last few decades, Jacobinism has lost its sheen, and in many countries there are demands that the state define itself as "pluri-national"—something that can take many different institutional forms. The problem here is to define the institutional forms and the "limits" of pluri-nationality. Merely asserting that a state is pluri-national does not solve the problem.

(3) **Democracy:** One of the great legacies of the French Revolution was to legitimize worldwide the concept that "sovereignty" belongs neither to a ruler nor to a legislature, but to the "people." The problem is that this concept, while rhetorically legitimate, terrifies those with power, prestige, and privilege. They seek to dilute the claim in every way possible.

As of the late twentieth century, there remained hardly any state that did not claim it was "democratic." Usually, the claim was based on the existence of national elections and a multi-party system. It is not difficult to show that holding such elections every several years and conferring representative power, even alternately, on parties that have only limited differences in actual programs scarcely exhausts the idea of popular sovereignty. Personally, I do not believe that there is any state today that meets my definition of democracy, although some are surely worse than others.

The struggle for democratization has become much more active and acute in the last half-century, with more and more groups insisting on increased real participation in decision-making. This is very positive, but a task just begun, far from being even half-finished.

(4) **Capitalism:** Our modern world-system is a capitalist system, based on the drive for the endless accumulation of capital. In terms of this criterion, it has been a quite successful system for the last 500 years. There has been constant growth in capital and continued concentration and centralization of the accumulators.

Like all systems of any variety, its processes fluctuate with some regularity—the cyclical rhythms of a system. The system survives because there are in-built mechanisms that force these fluctuations back to equilibrium, a moving equilibrium. Slowly but relentlessly, the processes move towards asymptotes. The secular trends reach points where the fluctuations move too far from equilibrium, and the system can no longer maintain the relatively stable environment in which it had normally operated.

When this happens, the system comes into terminal crisis. It bifurcates and becomes "chaotic." The struggle is no longer over the survival of the system but over which alternative prong of the bifurcation wins out and is the basis of a replacement system. We are in that period of systemic transition right now. We face another 20-40 years of struggle before the collective "decision" will have been made. It is intrinsically impossible to predict the outcome but it is very possible by our individual and group action to affect it. One possible outcome is a new system that replicates the worst features of the capitalist system—a system that is hierarchical, exploitative, and polarizing—with a non-capitalist system that is perhaps even worse. The other possible outcome is a system that is relatively democratic and relatively egalitarian, a kind of system the world has never known but is quite feasible.

Conclusion: We cannot assess the utility of political action within Turkey, within the Kurdish community, unless we place our analysis within the framework of these four contradictions: the continuing drive of the Turkish state to reinforce its sovereignty; the thrust of many in Turkey to employ and reassert the Jacobin option; the thrust of many to achieve greater democratization; and the ways in which all these kinds of political action will affect the worldwide struggle about what kind of system will replace the now doomed capitalist world-system.

Foreword

I offer this presentation because discussions on democratization in Turkey are intensifying and also because of the particular responsibilities that I hold. The year 2009 has become extremely important for the solution of the Kurdish question—the question at the heart of these discussions. As the Turkish president Abdullah Gül has said, "It shall be resolved—there is no other way." For me to make this presentation is even more important because the institutions concerned with state security have made clear statements on the urgency of the resolution of problems, and because of evaluations made about me in the public domain and the appeals made to me.

Other factors that influence this presentation are the written and verbal wishes of then-president Turgut Özal, at the beginning of the 1990s, and of then-prime minister Necmettin Erbakan in 1997; the briefing notes sent from the Army Social Relations Department at about the same period; discussions with certain authorities during and after the ten days of interrogation after my arrest in 1999; and letters I sent to various competent authorities and the tendency of the Republic of Turkey to be a bit more clear.

Part I: INTRODUCTION

There have always been questions regarding democratization. Contrary to what we might think, it is not a phenomenon that appeared with European modernity. Democratic tendencies have always been part of societies. Democracy is related to phenomena intrinsic to all beings: initiative, orientation and administration in relation to itself. I believe this is universal.

Throughout the history of civilization, especially at the beginning of the Sumerian times, assemblies consisting of spokespersons from rural and urban areas undoubtedly played a very important role. The first observable democratic institutions surfaced not in ancient Athens but in Sumerian cities. Over time, as the power and influence of priests, political administrators, and military officials within the administration increased, democratic institutions lost their significance and became of secondary importance. During the period of nimrods and pharaohs—the age of god-kings—ordinary people were construed as "created subjects." It was therefore no longer possible to even talk about democratic institutions. Nearly all civilizations went through similar periods. The Athenian democracy and the Roman republic were the final examples during antiquity.

In early Christianity—before it became the official religion of the Byzantine Empire—and in early Islam, the strong imperial tradition rapidly eliminated the influence of democratic elements and strictly centralized administration. At the beginning of the eleventh century, new urban institutions emerged in continental Europe that were long administered democratically. Towns were compelled to defend their independent democratic institutions against feudal authorities. Democratic elements also played an important role when princes and independent village (rural) societies resisted thriving kingdoms.

Starting in the early fifteenth century, the kingdoms turned into absolute monarchies. They sidelined democratic institutions substantially, just as they had done with traditional civilizations. Only the Magna Carta, formally imposed on England in 1216, preserved the existence of a democratic tradition. The 1789 Great French Revolution began as a popular revolution against the absolute monarchy, but in time it turned into the dictatorship of the bourgeoisie, which organized itself as the nation-state and gained authority that surpassed that of absolute monarchy. The small nation-states that multiplied as a result of the British Empire's divide-and-rule policies were used to construct a status quo. Despite their liberal ideals, all regimes operating as nation-states were in essence oligarchic regimes administered by elites. Existing parliamentary institutions were never able to eliminate the hegemony of the oligarchic elites. But nor could democratic institutions, based on the lasting struggles of urban and rural peoples, ever be eliminated either. Consequently, European democracy is a class phenomenon with limited popular content, and it is under the oligarchic control of the bourgeoisie. Since the 1950s, Europe has attempted to construct a confederation of democracies called the European Union (EU), which would surpass the nation-states. But to date the oligarchic monopoly of nation-states has not yet been broken. This attempt is important, but the chance of success is uncertain.

At the beginning of the nineteenth century, the Ottoman Empire, like the rest of the world, was influenced by the European powers and especially by the British Empire, which based its hegemony on the industrial revolution. The Ottoman Empire was constructed in the the old Middle Eastern state tradition. So as not to fall apart in the face of rapidly developing nation-states, it tried to centralize itself more tightly and renew itself bureaucratically. The Ottomans harshly suppressed internal rebellions. Ultimately the present Republic of Turkey, comprising Turks and Kurds as well as numerous other ethnic groups in Anatolia and northern Mesopotamia, was the offspring of this empire. The British Empire played a decisive role: at the beginning of the twentieth century, the Turkish bourgeoisie organized itself as the Union and Progress Party, made up of different nationalities. But during the Second Meşrutiyet[1] period and later during the Republican regime, it adopted a severe nationalism and turned into a dictatorship. Despite the presence of certain charismatic leaders like Mustafa Kemal Pasha, the bureaucratic oligarchic dictatorship preserved its existence to date. Numerous

1 Constitutional period in the Ottoman Empire between 1908-1922

state-oriented political parties and religious communities were established: legal and illegal, left and right, secular and religious. None of them was able to refrain from living and sustaining the institutional and ideological influence of the oligarchic autocracy. For a century an oligarchic autocracy has nested within the state. The present Ergenekon[2] trials, that deal with this traditions, are so important that its results shall determine the fate of Turkish democracy.

Democracy has been discussed in Turkey since not only the Meşrutiyet period but also since the Tanzimat[3] period, yet it remained undeveloped both theoretically and institutionally. Least of all did it ever really mean anything for the people. It was a game played mainly by the two major oligarchic groups, whose power bases lay with the rural artisans or within the state bureaucracy. These two elitist oligarchic groups repressed and crushed anything that truly came close to representing the interests of the people. The system's economic, ideological, political, military and cultural structure made it inaccessible to the people, as it remains to this day. But popular struggles have challenged this system, too, ever since its establishment, never more so than at present. Problems of democratization developed that were never adequately understood, due to the introverted character of the regime as well as to the strict nationalist, religious, sexist and positivist scientist ideologies it embodied. Law consisted simply of the rules of the state: individual and human rights were never given a chance. Whenever control was challenged, it was reestablished by coups. The system permitted freedom neither of speech nor of association. Hence freedom of expression and association that did not rest on a certain social consensus was frequently eliminated. Freedom of expression and association, the principal features of democratization, were not permitted for the oppressed classes, religious communities, and peoples. Whenever steps were taken to implement them, they were prevented by brazen written or unwritten laws.

These brazen written and unwritten laws were applied to the Kurds and Kurdistan most stringently and enforced ruthlessly. The goal was to eradicate everything related to being Kurdish and to Kurdistan. The

2 Ergenekon is a clandestine, kemalist, ultranationalist organization in Turkey with ties to the military, security forces, politicians and media.

3 Reform period in the Ottoman Empire, 1838-76.

official ideology denied the existence of the Kurdish people, who were to be eliminated through physical punishment and through profound and comprehensive assimilationist programs. Starting in the 1970s, when many other groups around the world formed to oppose oppression and called themselves leftist, a group calling itself the PKK initiated a resistance that has endured till now, the year 2009. This resistance has gone through various stages and endured great suffering and losses. Nonetheless it has played a significant role in exposing problems associated with democracy and in suggesting the solutions to these problems.

On the other hand, the United States and European Union, due to developments that threaten their interests, are at present avoiding oligarchic imposition and are now more receptive to democratic solutions. All these issues increase, for the first time, the chances for a democratic solution within Turkey. The overriding need is for a new civilian constitution, based on a social consensus, that guarantees fundamental individual and social rights, including freedom of expression and the right to democratic association. Such a constitution will make possible and guarantee the democratic, social, secular and juridical attributes of the Republic.

It will also make it possible to find solutions for not only the Kurdish question but all problems in Turkish society. A republic that allows Kurds to have individual and social rights will not lead to secession; on the contrary, it will allow a true and permanent democratic unity, by reinforcing the position of one of the fundamental partners and historically one of the republic's founding groups. It will free the Republic of severe trauma, pain and suffering, and end the loss of human life and property. It will make permanent the security of the country and people and their development and happiness.

Part II: CONCEPTS, THEORETICAL FRAMEWORK AND PRINCIPLES

In order to achieve democratization and a solution to the Kurdish question, Turkey must clearly define certain concepts. As we proceed to prospective solutions, we too must lay out our conceptual framework and binding principles. We must clarify whether certain problems are temporary, periodic, or structural. If our solutions are of a temporary or periodic nature, and do not address structural problems, then those problems may recur. Some problems, for instance, can be solved by regulation and legislation, but structural and constitutional problems cannot: since they relate to the constitutional system, they require constitutional solutions.

A — CONCEPTS

In Turkey, until recently, arguments over certain problems would reach deadlock simply because defining the problem was prohibited. The concept of Kurd, for example, was prohibited, as were many left-wing concepts. The notion of Kurdistan still inspires fear, and official circles are still reluctant to use it. But the notion of Kurdistan has an empirical basis: it originated in the attributes of real local people, and the Seljuk and Ottoman administrations both used the word to mean "land of the Kurds". At the founding of the Republic, Mustafa Kemal Pasha often used the terms Kürdistan mebusu (deputy of Kurdistan), Kürdistan meclisi (assembly of Kurdistan), and Kürdistan vilayeti (province of Kurdistan). The subsequent prohibition of the concepts of Kurds and Kurdistan cannot eradicate their validity. If we wish to resolve the structural problem, then prohibiting the use of the words Kurds and Kurdistan will lead us to an impasse. So will the attribution of any other meaning to these concepts. Another concept that must be defined clearly is democratization, today one of the most distorted concepts in

Turkey. Democratization, in my judgment, is not class-based. It refers to all social contexts and bears the mark of no class or stratum. It denotes the safeguarding of freedoms of speech and association, as well as the rights of individuals of all social strata—be they a minority or a majority, and regardless of language, religion, ethnicity and nationality—against the state. The issue is not to either suspend the state within democracy or democracy within the state. Both have a different role and function. One of the most vital issues of democratization is the ability of state and democracy to counterbalance each other.

Two other important concepts that need to be clarified are republic and nation-state. Not all republics are nation-states—for example, the ancient Roman republic. The concept of republic, which is related to democracy, suggests an administration that represents all members of the public, regardless of social status, and is thus not tied to an oligarchic monopoly. A nation-state, on the other hand, is based on the analogy between state and nation. The most obvious examples are fascist Italy, Nazi Germany, and Imperial Japan. It denies the existence of different interest groups within a nation as well as their rights and freedoms. It does not allow groups within a state and nation to have different and contradictory interests. It is essentially a dictatorship, and no formal democratic veneer can change this fact. Therefore, as we proceed toward a solution in Turkey, it is critically important that the concepts of republic and nation-state be defined and understood correctly. The Kurdish question can be resolved within a republic, but it cannot be resolved within a nation-state, which amounts to the negation of a republic.

The concepts common homeland and nation must also be clarified. Peoples from different cultures may well regard the same geographical area as their common homeland, as history shows. For example, areas that today are called Turkey and Kurdistan were previously called Anatolia and Mesopotamia. They are the common homeland of many peoples, such as Turks, Kurds, Armenians, Assyrians, Arabs, Jews, Christians, and Greeks, as well as groups of Caucasian origin. It is neither fair nor realistic to view this land as the exclusive homeland of Turks and Kurds. Just because the borders of the Republic of Turkey encompass this area, it cannot be said to belong solely to the Turkish ethnicity.

Similarly, the concept of common nation. A nation is not composed merely of each and every citizen; more important, it is the sum of peoples, i.e., the citizens who belong to the nation. It may also be understood as the nation of nations. By consensus of those in the common homeland, the common nation includes all peoples who live within the borders of the same state, who make up the nation of that state. It would serve democratization better to name those who live in Turkey "the nation of Turkey," just as Turkey is officially called "the Republic of Turkey" and its parliament "the Grand National Assembly of Turkey."

Clarifying the concept of identity would also contribute to the solution. Identity refers to a community's feeling of belonging and to attributes such as religion, ethnicity, culture, and gender. But the important issue is whether the concept of identity is open and flexible or strict and firm. Being open and flexible about identity would make a tremendous contribution to achieving democratic solutions. Strictness and rigidity, on the other hand, will make the solution more difficult than necessary. It is possible to view the cross-breeding of identities as a form of prosperity. What is important to understand is that this approach is far different from the assimilation of one identity into another.

In general, when it comes to concepts, the most important point is not to fetishize them. One must not misrepresent a given social phenomenon or concept by exaggerating it or giving it an unrealistic, chauvinistic form. For instance, an insistence on defining the concepts of nation, country, religion, and language as fundamental dogmatic values is incompatible with the spirit of democratic solutions.

B — THEORETICAL FRAMEWORK

A clear theoretical framework for democratization will contribute to the solution. The most important fundamental issue is for us to theoretically distinguish nation-state and democratic nation. A nation-state requires the homogeneity of citizens with a single language and single ethnicity. It binds citizens to this belief by conditioning them to carry out certain rituals. Adherence to this belief is not patriotism; rather, it is chauvinistic nationalism and religionism. The nation-state disapproves of social differences, insisting on their sameness, as fascist ideology did. By contrast, a democratic nation is multilingual, multireligious, multiethnic, and multicultural, encompassing groups and individuals with different interests. It does not base itself on the sameness of citizens and groups. It rejects the equation between state and nation, viewing each as different formations. State and democracy will be elaborated presently; the important thing to note here is that when these two areas recognize each other's legitimacy, they become separate entities in equilibrium. This should be the constitution's most fundamental provision. A democratic nation considers groups, religious communities, and civil society to be as important as the citizen and constitutionally secures their existence. The concept of abstract citizen is nothing but liberal babbling. The citizen can gain a concrete meaning only by belonging to a group, community, or civil society.

The other important theoretical question is constitutional: Does the state or the individual underlie the constitution? This issue is much debated. A constitutional theory that a sum of rules regulates the state is much different from a constitutional theory that regulates the individual's rights and freedoms before the state. The same is true for collective rights and freedoms. Democratization must base itself upon the constitutional theory that implicitly protects individual and collective rights and freedoms before the state. The state, which is the most organized power, does not need protection—its very existence is already the expression of such protection. Limiting its operation to fundamental rules does not contradict the theory of democratic constitution.

The other important distinction to be thoroughly understood is the distinction between statist and democratic solutions to social issues. Statist theory regards the nationalization of all things to be the solution of all social issues. For example, even religion, which is related to metaphysical philosophy and belief, becomes a state property, a problem instead of a solution. Many economic, social, cultural and national problems are presumed to be resolved once they are a property of the state or are controlled by the state. Clearly this theory cannot resolve problems but multiplies and aggravates them. Democratic solution theory is based on an understanding that problems belong to the society and not to the state. Thus it follows that the solution must come from the relevant social unit. The more the relevant social unit asserts its freedoms of expression and association, the more reinforcement its solution will get. Statist theory would continually impose rules on society, whereas democratic theory affirms the importance of society's own initiative as well as its right to determine and construct itself. Its relationship with the state need not be based on either complete rejection or complete acceptance. Although tension and conflicts may emerge in their relationship, it requires coexistence in reconciliation and peace. In this context, the democratic solution is also related to peace. Not all peacemaking may regard a democratic solution as so pivotal. But all democratic solutions secure "honorable peace." Honorable peace can be achieved only when the sides making the peace acknowledge one another's existence and fundamental rights.

Another drawback of the statist theory is that it leads to the mentality that one can oppose a state only with another state. Democratic theory, by contrast, counters that it is neither necessary nor mandatory to form a counter nation-state. Democratic theory proposes a flexible solution that is not state, which does not seek to become a state and it neither rejects nor denies the state.

A further fundamental theoretical question relates to the theory of individual and collective rights. A tremendous amount of speculation on this issue is distorted by liberal individualism. A minimal understanding of social sciences shows us that what is individual is also social and that what is social is also individual; the one bears the other within itself. Individualism means nothing if there is no sociality—that's easily proven. Nor does it require any sophistication to understand that society is composed of individual efforts and relationships. The problem arises when liberalism, in order to be able to create a homogeneous nation and citizen, rejects group, religious community, and civil society rights. But the more one strips these collectives of their freedoms and rights, the more one increases the possibilities for capitalist and nation-state monopolies to achieve maximum exploitation and power. Affirming individual rights but not collective rights and in fact the total rejection of collective rights is a fascistic approach. Recognition of individual rights and freedoms is worthless in the absence of recognition of collective rights and freedoms. It is not even theoretically possible—it is a big swindle. For instance, to say "you can enjoy Islam as an individual but not socially" is fascist demagogy, as well as a trick to take back the right that is being given. Individual and collective rights and freedoms are inseparable and complement each other. The fundamental criteria for individual and collective rights and freedoms are the rejection of all extreme religious communities and collectives that deny the individual as well as the rejection of all extreme individualism that denies society.

As we develop the theoretical framework for the resolution of democratization issues, we need to understand that some of the most important problems emerged from European positivist social scientism, especially from France. Even though France is in its Fifth Republic, it still experiences problems related to secularism, citizenship and religious communities. It has lost its hegemonic claims, not only vis-a-vis the British Empire but in all of Europe and the world. Positivist social scientism has been the decisive factor. The Republic of Turkey, the previous Tanzimat period, and both Meşrutiyet periods based themselves upon France's Third Republic. Moreover they embraced French positivism, as it was then the ideology of modernity. Therefore it is quite important to examine the role it played and its outcome. Frankly, unless we clarify the practical impact of French positivism and its republican practices, we have no prospects for a successful solution of Turkey's democratization process, and old problems will persist. I am not talking about a total rejection of the impact of French positivism and its republican practices. But if we are not able to overcome its negative effects and benefit from the scientific revolution and developments in the theory of democracy since the 1950s, then we will miss an opportunity for grand democratization and freedom of thought.

The French influence on theory and praxis thus requires analysis. In general, presently, Eurocentric social sciences draw much criticism. The mask of orientalism in relation to the Middle East has gradually been pulled off. In short: We cannot ignore the Middle East's leading cultural values over the last fifteen thousand years and especially not the fact that they played a leading role in the main civilizations of the last five thousand. Nor can we ignore the opportunities for finding a solution in them. We cannot resolve or understand our fundamental social problems through a five-hundred-year-old vulgar materialist and positivist culture, and to try to do so may lead us to unsound structures. What is right, however, is to break loose from Eurocentric ideological hegemony and to place the tremendous human values and approaches present in the Middle Eastern and Far Eastern traditions back on the agenda for resolving social problems. If we are to talk about a model for Turkey or the Middle East, it should emerge from these great historical and social realities.

Positivist philosophy, contrary to its claims, has led to the most stringent dogmatism. In the name of being scientific, it has legitimized the dogmatism of modernity and paved the way for a fanaticism of faith that is more unyielding than religion. For instance, the meaning it attributes to the concepts of nation, country, state, society, etc., is more rigorous than the one attributed to the concept of God. It exalts these concepts as deities that are stronger than God. Consequently, it deprives them of their true content. By making generalized statements about things outside the scope of a particular truth, one reduces the validity of that truth. Objectification leads to a more dangerous dogmatism than subjectification. The wars of the last five hundred years, and the worldwide approach to the limits of sustainability in many areas, are closely linked to positivist materialism.

But as we try to avoid objective dogmatism, we are not opting for subjective dogmatism. Our priority should be to get rid of the ideological hegemony of the West. Only then will it be possible to give social problems, and especially democratization, the attention they deserve, in accordance with their own social nature. A lasting democratization can be attained only if it is discussed in an environment of total intellectual freedom and in accordance with its social nature. Eurocentric sociological concepts and theories cannot analyze the extraordinary layers of cultural heritage (including that of Islamic culture). The orientalist implementations of the last two hundred years have sufficiently demonstrated this reality. The "Israel-Arab" conflict alone indicates the extent of the deadlock. The concepts of Israel and Arab, as positivist nation concepts, are themselves mechanisms that generate problems. The more one attributes meaning and value to being Israeli and Arabic, the more the question becomes complicated. This is because neither concept, Arab or Israeli, stands up to reality and gives us true meaning.

We may propose a similar approach to the concepts of being Turkish and Kurdish. The more value and meaning we ascribe to being Turkish and Kurdish, the more we aggravate the problems that have formed around these concepts. Turkishness and Kurdishness are realities that gained weak factuality mostly in the last century. Exalting such a weak factuality (that should have remained as such) to the level of much exaggerated fact led to a severe complication of the problems. Nationalism, as a positivist religion, aggravates social problems more than do traditional religions. Briefly then, theories of democratization can contribute to realistic solutions only if they can break away from objective and subjective dogmatism.

An additional issue that needs to be considered theoretically is the relationship between historicity and now, the present. Here objective dogmatism, inspired by positivism, shows its greatest impact. It considers "now" to be a strictly deterministic quantitative accumulation of history, or it considers history to be a quantitative accumulation of "now" going back in time. Indeed, it does not see a difference between history and now. Therefore it rejects history. To claim that "now is history" creates a terrible web of errors and mistakes. Besides, the positivist construction of now is built on a 90 percent denial of the truth. Its impact on history leads either to serious denial or to its counterpart, exaggeration.

It is more appropriate to determine, through thorough research, how history conditions the now (the present). No social problem can be treated and solved in the absence of its historical background or by turning it upside down. We must talk about a now in a way that reflects its history. Just as it is correct to search for the present in history, it is also correct to search for history in the present. But history is not the present—there are clear conditions between them. What is dangerous is to deem them identical without correctly evaluating those conditions. We must then bow before our fate. If this were so, we would have no need to understand any given issue nor any chance for a solution. We need to consider the present as an opportunity for a solution, provided that its terms are found within historical truths. Just as it is important and necessary to see the strict conditioning between them, seeing their differences is correct and contributes to the solution.

A final contribution to the theoretical framework should come from thinking and practices grounded in religion and morality. Democratization understood solely within the framework of political theory would be both unfair and unconscionable. Society is not only a political reality; it is also a moral and religious reality. For thousands of years, religion and morality as institutions focused on social problems and developed solutions. Developing analyses and generating solutions based solely on economic and political realities but overlooking these indispensable historical institutions will inevitably render them insufficient and mistaken. Attempting to resolve issues with such an approach would lead to the aggravation of issues.

One of positivism's most devastating effects on society is that it minimizes the role of religion and morality in solving problems. Eastern and Middle Eastern cultures have extracted religious and moral judgments from thousands of years of social experience in analyzing and resolving issues according to justice and conscience. It is necessary to refer back to them. Orientalism, by invalidating these traditional ways of solving problems, has aggravated democratic problems and increased despotic repression. Social life cannot be sustained if there is no justice and conscience. Strictly economic-deterministic and power-centered approaches that are reduced to the ice-cold interests of capital can give rise only to uncontrollable situations. More often than not, they do.

Inevitably we must turn to justice and conscience in order to democratically solve our vast social problems. Consider peoples like the Armenians and Assyrians: their economic, political, and military power was insufficient to overcome the tragedies they experienced. A return to conscientious and just judgments of religion and morals, always present in the region's culture, is necessary to help them out of the situation in which capitalist modernity has placed them.

C — PRINCIPLES

We must develop our framework of principles, using the theoretical framework as basis. Our democratic solution must not merely be topical, in accordance with the current political situation. For the solution to be permanent, it must be structural. Resolving the problems should contribute to re-construction; it should not just salvage today's system. Such solutions are essential in order to have a functional state and lasting social stability. Democracy is a system of state and society, and thus democratization must proceed systematically. The principles I list below, which can be added to, are the minimum conditions for achieving a democratic system.

1. Democratic Nation Principle

A nationhood that brings unity should not be a nation-state—rather, it should be a democratic nation. Existing nationhoods must aim to transform themselves into a democratic nation. A sufficient point of departure for this objective might be open cultural identities and flexible nationality. The nationhood within which unity is to be achieved must be constructed not forcefully by the rulers but on the basis of democratic willingness. In a democratic nation, individual and collective rights and freedoms complement one another. A democratic nation not only embodies the citizen but values civil society and religious groups and peoples as a source of wealth. The more citizens are elements of a functioning collective, the stronger will be their position.

2. Common (Democratic) Homeland Principle

A common (democratic) homeland would be made up of multilingual, multinational and multireligious citizens, rather than a single ethnicity with one language and one religion. This would much better fulfill the requirements of unity and fraternity. A homeland comprised of a single ethnicity will alienate the majority of citizens, set them apart as different, as other than the dominant ethnicity. Such alienation increases polarization and is the real separatist. The notion of a uniform citizenry is clearly of fascist origin. Diversity is the wealth of both nature and society. Patriotism should not be based on chauvinism and racism; rather, it should be cherished as a commitment felt for the soil, for ecology, and for development.

3. Democratic Republic Principle

A republic is a type of state. But seeing the republic as a nation-state—especially strict nation-state forms—leads to the separation of peoples.

The ideal state for a republic is not a nation-state but a democratic state. A state cannot simultaneously be a nation-state and a democratic state—they are mutually contradictory. A democratic state is receptive to a democratic system and can be reconciled with it. A nation-state has no such aim; on the contrary, it assimilates democratic society. The democratic solution principle is compatible with republic but not with nation-state. The important thing is to envisage and construct the republic as the umbrella organization for democratization, for all citizens. When developing a democratic solution, the republic should not be ideological or tied to a single ethnicity or religion. It is critical to define the republic as the organization of democratic laws for all citizens. Social and secularist principles would be embodied concisely within the definition of the republic. By clearly defining the republic, we avoid tying it to a single ethnicity, religion, or ideology. For instance, the republic would be more complete and united if concepts such as Turkishness and Kurdishness (which embody ethnicity and race) as well as attributes such as Islam, Christianity, and Sunnism (which are religious and ideological terms) are not included in the definition.

4. Democratic Constitution Principle

Democratization is a political movement; it cannot be a permanent and systematic governing regime unless it is based on a constitution formed by consensus within society. Democratic constitutions denote the reconciliation between democratic society and the state. Individual rights and freedoms can become meaningful only within a democratic society. In the absence of a constitution, people cannot be protected against the state because of the enormous concentration of power in the state. A democratic constitution is an indispensable tool to keep the state an entity of expertise and accumulated experience for the purposes of attaining solutions and not as an institution that aggravates and generates problems. A democratic constitution is the adhesive that holds society and state together. It does so by keeping the state not only functional but specifically an entity for the accumulation of expertise and experience.

5. Democratic Solution Principle

Civil society, democratized, will aim to become neither a state nor an extension of it. It does not seek fundamental changes within the state; instead, it seeks a functional democratic regime within society. It demands at most a democratic constitution from the state. But making a democratic constitution should be satisfactory, based on social well-being and not on the state. The opposite of the democratic solution principle is the imposition of power-centered and statist solutions. As a principle, democratic solution does not deal with power sharing—in fact, it keeps itself away from power. The more intense power gets, the further away one gets from democracy. If societies are arranged in the name of governments and states alone, then the resulting order will be antidemocratic because of the exclusion of social forces. If arrangements made by the ruling power and government are constructive, then it may pave the way for democratization, but it does not constitute democratization itself. The goal of democratic solutions cannot be the sharing of power or state resources. Getting hold of the state and becoming a part of the state cannot be the aim of democratic solution.

The democratic solution principle seeks fundamentally to constitutionally safeguard the peaceful coexistence of democratic institutions and state institutions. The two institutional entities have a legal legitimacy. Neither bases its existence on the denial of the other. Democracy does not need to eliminate the state; nor should the state dissolve democracy for its benefit. The extreme intertwinement of the two within the Western system transforms democracy into a showcase institution. One of the most urgent problems of democratization is to overcome this intertwinement and rearrange the coexistence of these two institutional entities. Just as democracy restricts the state, the state, as the accumulation of experience and expertise, functions as an umbrella to democracy. Democratic society will prevail in time. In brief, the peaceful but tense positioning of state and democratic institutions will lead to competition that will develop and strengthen the democratic society itself.

6. Inseparability of Individual and Collective Rights and Freedoms Principle

When the principle of rights and freedoms is implemented in order to resolve problems of democratization, a separation between individual and collective rights aggravates these problems and creates deadlock. Such a distinction goes against the nature of society. Never has an individual within a human society, free or not, existed in the absence of community. Therefore attaining rights and freedoms means nothing unless they are shared with the communities to which the individual belongs. An individual isolated from society is meaningless. Consequently, the rights and freedoms that the individual attains are as meaningless and cannot be implemented. The opposite is also true: the rights and freedoms given to collectives have no value if individual members do not benefit from them. Rights and freedoms cannot be enjoyed without the existence of the individual. Leaving the individual without rights and freedoms is leaving the collective to which he/she belongs destitute of rights and freedoms. Again, the opposite is true: If a collective is left destitute of rights and freedoms, then its individuals are in the same position. In short, rights and freedoms cannot be enjoyed if they are not shared. They cannot exist without the individual or the collective.

7. Ideological Independence and Freedom Principle

In order to achieve democratization and to become free, we must get rid of the ideological hegemony of capitalist modernity. Despite its vulgar materialist attributes, it is essentially idealist and poses as "positivist science." We must overcome this ideological hegemony. Positivist scientism is the dominant principle of European hegemonic civilization. In the absence of this principle, it cannot construct and administer capitalism, industrialism, and nation-statism around the world. It conquers minds in the Middle East with orientalist science. Conquest, occupation, and colonization occur in a variety of ways, always in cooperation with local despots. That worsens problems of democratization. Any resistance to it has elements of democracy. In order for these democratic elements to develop, become strong, and become systematized, they need to break away from hegemonic ideology. Any meaningful alternative ideological options must be local, urban, regional and multinational and correspond to a common homeland. Otherwise, a different ideological hegemony may develop.

Traditional religious and racist points of view are as hegemonic as the positivist hegemony of capitalist modernity. Ideological efforts based on advocacy of freedom can be called ideologies of freedom. Once we understand this, we can understand democratization problems and their solutions. Without ideological freedom, democratization can stumble or fall under the control of hegemonic ideologies. Ideological freedom is linked to the truth of social nature. It constantly expresses itself in the realization and enjoyment of democratic society. Social truth is the free expression of the realities of democratic society.

8. Principle of Historicity and Present

The problem democratization and its solutions are closely linked to the relations between historicity and the present. If we ignore problems experienced in history and their possible solutions, we cannot possibly understand democratization or any other social problem. Inevitably, an ahistorical mentality aggravates the problems, turning them into deadlock, crisis, conflict, or war. Historical events created the fundamental conditions that determine the present. The present is the part of history that presents itself with problems and possible solutions. We cannot intervene with the past, but we can intervene with the present. We can change the present, depending on the intervention's intellectual foundations and material power. We can speed up the present, change its direction, and make it more free or enslaved, depending on the forces that intervene. But the important thing is to answer the question "How should the history be reflected in the present?" We should analyze the present as the expression of history. This will be the key to resolving social problems. As we begin to understand history better, it will become the greatest source of our power. Those who cannot understand their history correctly cannot understand the present, let alone try to democratize it. Freedoms and democratizations that are discovered through trial and error cannot be permanent; they can be lost in the same manner as they were gained.

Society is the most advanced history. This reality must be understood; otherwise we cannot free society of its problems or provide democratic solutions. For this reason, the very first thing the despots do is eliminate social memory, and thus the very first thing democrats must do is protect social memory, or history. Capitalist modernity tries to destroy human memory and present the present as if it were eternal or, rather, the end of time. Accordingly, everything consists of the compressed present. The disease of individualism relates to this understanding of the present. The maxim "Live your own life, all else is meaningless" is linked to the denial of historical memory. Such a mentality will not deliver social truth or the democratic socialism that expresses it. Hence liberal individualism is the negation of democracy. It is a principle of social science to identify the instant in history and history in that instant.

9. Morality and Conscience Principle

Western sociology does not respect the principle of conscience. It operates on analytical intelligence, while conscience requires emotional intelligence. Modern sociology, which first began as analytical philosophy, has nowadays become an administrative technique. Conscience has brought society into existence; it functions as society's natural justice; and when it is ignored, society functions as a most dangerous, monstrous machine. Conscience is the essence of religion and morality. Stripping religion and morality of their dull traditional aspect, we see that social conscience remains. Social conscience is the area where those without political, military and economic power can take refuge. When this area is damaged, the principle of power will be the only principle in operation, and each will be a wolf to the other.

Democracy cannot function in the absence of conscience. Monopolist power and systems of capital, on the other hand, are built upon the repudiation of conscience. Democratization is the movement to invalidate this repudiation and to regain social conscience. The society outside the monopoly of power and capital can be defended only with a movement of conscience. Social struggle today is the struggle to regain lost conscience. If democratization does not acquire the lost values of conscience, then it cannot reach its full meaning. Individuals and minorities will not be able to attain their rights and freedoms. Thus the principle of conscience is the refined social value of religion and morality and must be part of the democratization solution.

Facts of genocide cannot be analyzed without resorting to conscience. Humanity can admit to all the murders and genocides of capitalist modernity and find justice for them only if the principle of conscience is activated. Modernity is based on the principle that power can solve social problems. Those that have power sort things out, and those who don't are no longer relevant. This disease, present in the foundations of modernity, leaves society in disarray. If we have any desire to find a lasting and fair response to social problems and especially to democratization, then we must definitely replace the principle of power with the principle of conscience. The culture of the East has given this principle prominence in dealing with all its problems. We cannot abandon this principle for the sake of the ice-cold interests of capitalism and power. As we develop solutions to Turkey's problems with democratization, we need to give the principle of conscience priority over all the other principles.

10. The Principle of Self-Defense in Democracies

No living beings, not even single-celled organisms, are without self-defense. This has been scientifically proven. No human society can exist without self-defense. Wars arise from the distorted understanding of self-defense systems of civilizations. Democratic societies and their free individuals face huge defense problems when trying to protect themselves in class-based civilizations. Primitive societies not only had conflicts amongst one another but faced deadly dangers posed by nature. Thus, at any given time and place, self-defense has been the foremost important duty.

Self-defense is a priority against the elements of capitalist modernity, due to the monopolist oppression and exploitation of the nation-state, capitalism, and industrialism against economy, ecology, and democratic society (including its free and equal individuals). The absence of self-defense not only results in wage enslavement, it paves the way for all kinds of unemployment, disease, and degeneration. Worse still, it carries numerous physical and cultural genocides within itself. Modernity in general compels society and individuals, but it also requires democratic societies and free individuals to defend their own existence. If they fail to defend themselves, they will lose not only their freedom but their existence. The monopolist elements of modernity, in order to sustain themselves, threaten the freedom and existence of society and the individual. Later they deplete the environment that is vital for life itself. The depletion of the environment is a type of genocide.

Democratic society and free individuals must find remedies not only for revolutionary and evolutionary developments but also for the problems of self-defense. The structural crisis of modernity has placed self-defense at the top of all other problems. Each community must be not only an economic, ecological, and democratic unit but also a unit with its own self-defense. Each equal and free individual may have to live in one or more communities that are economic, ecological, and democratic—and in a corresponding number of self-defense units. Nourishment, reproduction, and protection are the three indispensable conditions of living for all living beings, including human society.

Part III: THE PROBLEM OF DEMOCRACY AND THE SOLUTION OF DEMOCRATIC CONSTITUTION IN TURKEY

A — THE PROBLEM OF DEMOCRACY IN TURKEY

The problem of democracy arose when hierarchical administration emerged within tribal communities. This administrative separation terminated the tribal community's natural democracy. The transition from hierarchy to despotic state intensified this process, which essentially determined systems of civilization. Civilization had a limited amount of influence over society until capitalism emerged in Europe, but the moral and political potential of the society had preserved its strength. European civilization granted many privileges to the state and the nation-state, as they were part of capitalism and industrialism. But these privileges profoundly shattered and penetrated society. This penetration (which was really the ideological power and monopoly of capital) led to unprecedented domination. Modernity reduced the individual to its weakest state. Limited reforms tried to restrain the struggles that were waged. Through such reforms, European democracy tried to uphold the individual and society. The essence and framework of this democracy was individual rights and freedoms as well as the rule of law. The European Union is the systematized state of this foundation. But the monopolist state maintains its domination from the top, and the resulting democratic system can be nothing but a system of power that is highly constricted and kept under control. Alas, the problem of democracy continues to exist.

Around 7000 B.C. the glaciers in southern Siberia began to melt, and around 4000 B.C. the Siberian clans began to enjoy their Neolithic

Revolution, under the influence of the Middle Eastern Neolithic Revolution. The transition from hierarchy to civilization (i.e., to state) began around 2000 B.C., while the initial Chinese-centered civilization emerged around 1500 B.C. The clan prototypes of the present-day Japanese, Koreans, Vietnamese, Mongolians, and Turkestanis were in continuous struggle, in a democratic reaction against Chinese civilization. In Chinese historical records, the first reference to the ancestors of the Turks uses the name Huns. Hun clans enjoyed a primitive democracy and were thus in continuous conflict with Chinese civilization. They could not easily be civilized, and when they were placed under severe pressure, they headed for the West. The Western Huns lived in a large area that covered Central Europe to Rome around A.D. 400. But they were continually dissolved within other civilizations, by the Chinese in the East and by the Slavic-based civilizations in the West. The Hindu and Manichaeism religions tried to interrupt this process, but the real break came with Islam. The Göktürks and Uygurs tried to establish states around 550 and 740 respectively but went no further than being a confederation.

The civilization of the proto-Turks really began after the ninth century, when their contact with Islam developed. Problems associated with Turkishness and democratization began with the Karakhanid period; continuing till today, they are closely linked to this civilizational process. Middle Eastern Turkish-Islamic civilization is usually understood to start with Seljuk and his principality. Proto-Turks had earlier tried to make their mark within Middle Eastern civilizations, but the initial settlement of the masses and clans came with Seljuk and his sons. Seljuk himself faced two religious movements as he tried to find a homeland for himself: Judaism and Islam. The Judaic names given to his four sons suggest he was initially influenced by the Turkish state of Jewish Khazar. Thus one can only wonder how much of a Muslim he had become. It is possible to link Turkicization with Islam because, after the short-lived period of Göktürks, there are no other civilizations with a Turkish name. It was probably the Arabs who gave them this name. But before the era of nationalism, societies were identified not by their race but by their religion. One would be from Islam or another religion—that was how social reality was constructed.

The Seljuk principality aimed to establish strict hegemony over the clans it controlled from the eleventh century onward, but the clans strongly resisted. Some of the first Oghuz Turks that crossed over to Iran in 1017 complained about Seljuk's severity. This initial group of five thousand people fled to Iran for salvation. From the beginning those clans that crossed over to the Middle East seem to have shown strong resistance against a civilization based on urbanization, class division, and statehood. The tribal clans that were oppressed and enslaved were called Turkoman and are the nucleus of today's Turkic people. The aristocracy of the clans not only despised the Turkoman—they did not even want to call themselves Turks. They preferred titles such as shah and sultan and to be called Arab and Persian. They forgot Turkish. Linguistically, they used Arabic, Persian and an Ottoman Turkish, which is a mixture of them all. But the real Turkishness existed in the Turkoman clans.

Interpreting this brief history in relation to the problem of democracy brings us to the following conclusions:

Since the eleventh century, as Turkish clans crossed over to the Middle East, a serious class distinction began. This initiated the problem of democracy. Turkoman clans valued their freedom and democratic way of life, as can be seen in their treatment of the Sultan Ahmed Sanjar[4]—he was captured and carried around in a cage.

The core of the democracy problem in Turkey occurred after the adoption of Islam: the Turkish clans were divided into two fundamental groups. The military and religious aristocracy, as well as the landlords, were cozily ensconced within the state and monopolized power; the poor, in the cities and villages, were excluded from the system and lived like the old nomad clans or else sustained themselves with craftsmanship and farming. This separation, occurring among all Middle Eastern peoples, resulted in numerous rebellions and migrations. The divisions between denominations are related to this social division: Sunnism became the official denomination of the ruling strata, while oppositional

4 Ahmad Sanjar became the sultan of the Great Seljuk Empire in 1118. Oghuz Turks captured him in 1153 and held him until 1156. He died in 1157.

denominations like Alevism[5], Shi'ism, Illuminationism[6], Mawlawism[7], and Bektashism[8] continued in semisecrecy. These denominations struggled to attain democratization in the Middle Ages. Nomadic tribal life itself is a democratic struggle. In all the tribal orders of the Middle Ages, the essence of resistance was democratic struggle.

If official Islam was the ideological monopoly, then the semisecret denominational ideologies can be regarded as democratic discourse. These democratic popular movements functioned up until the early nineteenth century; they entered a new phase as capitalist modernity began to penetrate into the Middle East. The old imperial regimes disintegrated due to their inclination toward nation-states. On the other hand, the small nation-states that took over these old regimes further aggravated the problem of democracy. Nation-states embody a twofold alienation: that inherited from the previous civilization's political power, and that imposed by capitalist modernity. This increase in the monopoly of power imposed near-genocidal regimes on popular culture. The state simultaneously became capitalist, fascist, and bourgeois. In the twentieth century, Turkey comprehensively went through this process, as defined by the movement that called itself the Committee of Union and Progress.

The Committee of Union and Progress may well have been a prototype for both the Italian Fascist Party and the German National Socialist Party of the 1920s. Not by coincidence, countries that were late in becoming capitalistic experienced similar developments. This relates to the nature of capitalist modernity. The bureaucratic bourgeoisie calculated that it could emerge empowered from the deepening crisis of modernity if it carried out brutal class wars and genocides. Thus its responsibility in these wars was decisive.

At the same time one must not overlook the contribution made by the real socialist movement, which selected the nation-state and

5 Alevism is influenced by animism and Zoroastrianism more than by Islam, so it cannot really be considered a denomination of Islam. This is especially true for the Kurdish Alevis.

6 The school of Illuminationism, influenced by Avicennism and neo-Platonism, was founded by the philosopher Shahab al-din Suhrawardi (1155–91).

7 Mawlawism is a Sufi order founded by Jalal ad-Din Rumi.

8 Bektashism is a Sufi order that inherited numerous pre-Islamic Turkish beliefs.

industrialism elements of modernity as its primary goal. It was not only democracy that faced uncertainty—so did the existence of people as a cultural entity. The period between the two world wars, as well as the wars themselves, can be seen as a frenzy of capitalist modernity, which through its three main elements (capitalism, nation-statism, and industrialism) sealed its hegemony all over the world. Many nations, peoples, and cultures felt the threat of this frenzy to the bone. Even those who escaped could not refrain from overstating its importance and impact, and they thus surrendered themselves to the ruling system. The Third International could not transcend modernism. Its efforts to develop the popular and antifascist fronts in the 1930s did not contribute much to democracy. After the Second World War, the liberal democracy of the cold war period and real socialist popular democracy were both in essence negations of democracy. They continued their hegemonic warfare with a democratic gloss. The collapse of real socialism was at the same time the collapse of liberalism. After the 1990s, the world fell into in turmoil due to the system's deepening structural crisis. The democracy problem returned to the agenda with all its severity. There were efforts to redefine democracy in terms of its content and form and to systematize itself under democratic modernity.

In this turmoil, Turkey faced not only existential problems but also an opportunity to make a new beginning as a republic. In a sense, Mustafa Kemal Pasha and the Republic were identical entities; he was the historical personality that initiated that process. Understanding these two entities is still very important today. Mustafa Kemal said that he kept the idea of a republic secret until the appropriate day came to declare it. This gives rise to important questions. How was the Republic established and realized? From which universalities did it stem? These questions are still unanswered. Was it a democracy? If so, why are we in our current situation? These fundamental questions need to be answered truthfully if we are to understand the democracy problem that has brought Turkey to an impasse.

This subject cannot be clarified by looking only at recent history. As with different countries around the world, Turkey's situation is to be understood in relation to the rising hegemony of European civilization. While this hegemony increased, Europe was going through its most powerful phase of globalization, and it is thus not really helpful to examine developments in remote corner separate from this hegemonic system. Second, the transformations in Turkey may be connected with endeavors in Europe. Here the key concept is Jacobinism, which made its existence felt in all the revolutions of modernity, most profoundly within the French Revolution. Jacobinism must be well understood, because it had significant consequences in Turkey as well as other parts of the world.

First, Jacobinism appears to be a universal of modernity. It played a pivotal role in transcending the theocratic tradition that had left its mark on five thousand years of civilization. It represented the middle class, the bourgeoisie that aimed to come into power. It was the radical section of bourgeois revolutionism. It denoted both ideological radicalism and radical action. Its most appropriate conditions for attaining power were when there was an occupation by a foreign power. Without a clear occupation, Jacobinism could not come into power—its opportunity came only when the whole society felt threatened by such an explicit occupation. Such circumstances were conducive for Jacobinism to appear as a political power. Society was looking for a savior; the traditional rulers, the theocratic monarch, did not prevent the occupation but quickly entered into collaboration with the foreign occupiers, to protect their own interests. They suffered a serious loss of legitimacy within society. Apart from the collaborationist upper classes, the middle classes were the most suitable (ideologically and organizationally), and the Jacobin bourgeoisie were the best educated and organized. The earliest Jacobins appeared in the Dutch and English Cromwell led the biggest Jacobin revolution in England and decapitated the king in the 1640s, long before the French Revolution. Indeed, the biggest Jacobin revolution was not the one that occurred in France in 1792 but the one in England. France was the second or third version of this model.

In the Netherlands too Jacobinism fermented, albeit differently. It grasped power not only when the upper, traditional layer could no longer administer or govern, but also when the poor, lowest classes had no adequate ideological and organizational instruments. In all three countries, Jacobinism jumped to the forefront under similar conditions with the strongest libertarian, egalitarian, and independence slogans; under its leadership, it got the majority of society to rebel. The critical moment came when the majority of society rebelled for power. This was also the moment when the greatest changes were conceived and everything was shaken to the bone. For the birth of the new, this is necessary. This most critical moment for France began in April 1792. The collaborationist king was not only trying to realize a counterrevolution, in cooperation with all of the European aristocracies, but was also planning his escape. The middle-class moderates, the Girondists, were reluctant to take radical steps. The Babeuf communists were in the weakest position of all. The political atmosphere was quite suitable for the Jacobins, and under these conditions the worst reign of terror known to history began, ending only when the Jacobin leader Robespierre was sent to the guillotine in July 1794. Also during this period, 1792 to 1794, the first republican constitution was adopted. After 1794 all of the new periods were essentially part of the search for a new order. This pursuit continues today with the Fifth Republic.

Before we analyze Jacobinism, we need to understand, even if superficially, some of its fundamental points. First, it is not a minority movement but a popular one. Second, although it uses slogans about egalitarianism and freedom, it is essentially a radical movement to politically empower the middle class. It may also be called dictatorial. Third, when the country's internal and external threats disappear, the Jacobin movement loses the circumstances in which it can function and begins its decline. Usually right-wing forces fill the vacuum, but every now and then forces to its further left may do so, as occurred in the short-lived revolutions of 1848 and during the 1870 Paris Commune. When Jacobinism rebels, it declares itself a new and united nation; when it attains power, it declares itself a nation-state. This nation and nation-state are the name and form of the new divinity that replaces the universal, ecumene, and ummah[9] that were the traditional forms of society. The declared new nation and nation-statism are a new religion, perceived to replace the old one. In order to attain power, the Jacobins must formally declare society to be a new divinity; otherwise the old religious community can overthrow it. The inflexible birth of the French nation-statism was closely linked to the excessive terrorization of revolution, and this

9 Commonwealth of the Islamic believers.

terrorization of revolution is characteristic of middle-class radicalism. At times, it feels the need to be harsh and merciless in order to attain power; when the opportunity to come into power no longer exists, it rapidly becomes passive. When the conditions and hopes to attain power recede, those who surrender to the right-wing forces and rapidly fade away are once again the Jacobins. Only a minority of them become more radical and join the communists or transform into a communist movement. We see this cycle in all the revolutionary periods of Europe and later in the rest of the world. Another important point that needs to be clarified in the concrete example of Europe is the link between fascism, Bolshevism, and Jacobinism.

Jacobinism did not end in 1794—it left its mark, one way or another, on later revolutionary periods. It was the precursor of the two extremes: classes controlling political power and nationalism. Russian nationalism and Bolshevism also had Jacobin roots, as did German nationalism and its most extreme form, Nazism. The Jacobin roots of Italian fascism are even clearer. Nazism and Fascism—all fascisms—represent the most terrorist form of rule by the monopolized Jacobin bourgeoisie. On the other hand, Bolshevism (and similar movements) represents the terrorism of those who have attained power in the name of the lower classes. Both of them express and construct the nation and the nation-state in an extreme manner (albeit in the name of different classes). But undeniably they have common Jacobin roots.

An important issue that needs to be clarified is whether the Bolsheviks really became communists. I personally am of the opinion that the Bolsheviks, with their Jacobin roots, were not able to undergo a communist transformation. They were power-focused and were nationalists with a class perspective. Thus this led them to construct themselves as a nation-state. But the nation-state is the fundamental state regime of capitalism, which they were against. Pioneering industrialism makes them emerge as radical modernists. By now nothing remains of their revolution. The experience of real socialism especially in the Soviet Union and China confirms this fact.

The relationship between Jacobinism and liberalism is clearer. Jacobinism plays the role of liberalism's revolutionary terrorist movement, its radical wing. Liberalism is like an octopus; it works in many ways. The only two movements that liberalism has not incorporated within itself are Catholic philosophy and the democratic communalist movement.

The liberal point of view, as an ideological hegemony, is most difficult to analyze. It employs subjective and objective idealism and the materialism of the positivist ideology. It disintegrates within its own modernity movements and lifestyles. The disintegration of the anarchists as well as current feminist and ecological movements proves that the ideological hegemony of liberalism is a true source of power for capitalism.

Clearly the birth of modern Turkey should be analyzed in relation to the global and Jacobin attributes of capitalism. Capitalism made the transition to its imperialist monopoly phase in the 1870s. The Ottoman Empire was entering a period of disintegration, specifically with the treaty of Berlin in 1878. Nation-statist movements were weakening the old traditional imperial institutions both internally and externally, and the precautions taken to reform the empire were not effective, as the primary problem was to rescue the empire. Within the Ottoman Empire, the Young Turks were influenced by Mazzini's movement and took the form of Jacobinism's nationalist wing.

The Young Turks were a form of Ottoman nationalism, and their Committee of Union and Progress had several striking aspects. First, it organized itself within the state, not within society. Second, it organized itself as state nationalism from the outset. Third, the state facilitated the transformation of its own system into capitalism and bourgeoisie. These three characteristics reveal the right-wing and fascist characteristics of Union and Progress Jacobinism. Even German Nazism and Italian Fascism began as popular movements and later organized themselves as states. But Union and Progress came into being within the state. This reflects the most backward characteristic of Jacobin nationalism: it is a fascist characteristic that is actually no longer Jacobin. The fact that it organized itself as a parallel state within the state made it unique. It symbolizes the birth not of a progressive state but of a fascist state when compared to the traditional state. It is the first of its kind, an exemplary phenomenon. Not surprisingly, Hitler took it as a model. It was the initial model to establish a state within a state.

More bizarrely, this state nested within a state constructed a nationalism. The initial four people who founded the CUP were not of Turkish ancestry, but their attempt to construct a proto-Turkish nation heralded the democracy problem, which would become so severe. The parallel state that they constructed was in contrast with both the traditional state and with social facts. It was a total fabrication. Hence another distinct fascist characteristic introduced itself. At the beginning of the twentieth century, it headed for underground activity. The 1906 armed underground activity began the civil war within the state. The concept of a civil war within the state was interesting and unique. It later became a model for coup making, even in Western-style democracies.

To use the formal state as an informal nucleus is the most severe violation of democracy. Worse still, the state ceases to be a state. One of the most obvious features of the state is its official character and its administration of society according to certain rules. Despite all their flaws, the Ottoman sultans administered the state using distinct traditions. They had certain morals and rules, albeit of religious character. Conspiracies were seldom employed as a tactic and were only possible as personal acts. But the Union and Progress's administrative style for state and society was conspiratorial and had the attributes of a coup. Ceasing to be a state defines this reality. As the First World War began, this reality came directly into play. The most degenerate and fascist methods of Jacobinism did not rescue the state but eliminated it. Stated differently, the state became extinct and turned into a gang. The first and second mesrutiyet, despite all its good intentions, contributed to a ganglike and anticonstitutionalist state or a no-state situation, contrary to its aims. The bureaucratic banditry of the new state made everyone yearn for the old one.

The defeat of German fascism in 1945 was similar to the defeat of Union and Progress fascism in the name of Turkishness in 1918. It could not have happened any other way. The gangs had long ago defeated the state. In 1918 not only the state but society as well faced a clear occupation in Anatolia and Mesopotamia. The crisis of state and democracy was experienced most profoundly, and the remaining state instruments and social forces had no option but to defend themselves. In the face of these events, Mustafa Kemal's leadership had Jacobin characteristics: the blatant foreign occupation continued, the traditional ruling elite collaborated with the foreign powers, and the very weak communist movement was unprepared to lead society. The only ones that might lead it were the middle class, who would mobilize in the name of the whole of society and were the most radical and organized. Kemal, due to his personality and upbringing and with his self-consciousness and will power, was cut out for this job. He also knew French and thus could understand the Third Republic's embrace of the principles of Jacobinism. He understood the Jacobin republicanism quite well. His position was organizationally important as well: he opposed the Union and Progress administration. After it broke up, he formed his own group, which contributed much to his becoming a Jacobin leader. Thereafter he needed to make the transition to being an actual leader.

How Mustafa Kemal became an actual leader in 1919 is widely known. The fundamental question is how he managed to surmount the British occupation and Sultan Mehmed VI. There was much speculation about it, but as he made the transition to being an actual leader, they lost their importance. The declaration of the Grand National Assembly of Turkey in 1920 was not only taken in opposition to the occupation; it was a social revolution. The assembly's features and objectives prove this.

Social forces, not dispersed state forces, played a pivotal role in this revolution. The state instruments were profoundly defeated and unfit; if the social forces had not supported them, they could not have commanded the revolutionary movement. Mustafa Kemal seems to have had a good grasp of the situation and thus insisted that the assembly was to be the only source of legitimacy. Although the assembly may not have had adequate depth in understanding the issues, it was aware of the conditions of the revolution. It represented the majority of the forces present within society. The democratic attributes of the first assembly were apparent. Its religious, national, and class structure clarified its position in relation to the 1920 National Pact. It would oppose occupation to the end. The religious features of society were more prominent than its national features. The Muslim Turks and Kurds were the main social forces and were not hostile to communism. Through Kemal's friendship with Lenin, the assembly was on good terms with the Communist International. It carried the mark of the middle class. An important section of the bureaucracy and gentry belonged to this class and saw the movement as the remedy for the critical situation. The alliance in the Grand National Assembly of Turkey consisted of three main forces: the middle class (represented by secular Turkish nationalists), the proponents of the Islamic ummah (represented by Turkish and Kurdish leaders from the gentry and the tribes), and the common people (represented by socialists who sympathized with Bolsheviks). Under the occupation, these movements and their leaders mobilized themselves as social forces.

It took a while before the leadership of Mustafa Kemal was acknowledged. Violence and military actions dominated the revolutionary period from 1920 and 1922. It really was a Jacobin period and created an important opportunity for democratization. This opportunity gained further promise with the declaration of the republic in 1923. But the 1924 constitution fell far short of the 1921 constitution; the 1923 elections suppressed the rich representation in the Grand National Assembly of Turkey; and the Kurds were excluded, on the pretext of the 1925 Kurdish rebellion. All of this reversed the historical opportunity in favor of a single-party hegemonic system.

Why and how this transition was made is still an open question. In January 1921, the leader of the Turkish Communist Party (TKP), Mustafa Suphi, and other leading cadres were killed; in 1923, Said-i Nursî and Mehmet Akif [Ersoy], two important figures of the Islamic movement, were sent to exile; and numerous conspiracies and provocations were made against the 1925 Kurdish rebellion. Whoever was behind these incidents, no matter what their reasons were, they destroyed the democratic alliance and gave rise to the hegemonic period. If we hold Mustafa Kemal responsible for the hegemonic period, we may lose sight of its real cause. Mustafa Kemal had adequately played his historical role by preventing the occupation and declaring the Republic. But he was unable to protect the democratic alliance of the Republic or stop its deterioration. Internal and external factors were more effective in this respect than the role played by the individuals. Internally those inciting the Kurdish Rebellion and those collaborating with the sultanate played an important role in excluding the Kurds. The Grand National Assembly of Turkey, however, had already in 1922 accepted the establishment of an assembly based on autonomy for Kurds, in a secret vote of 373 to

63. At the beginning of 1924, Mustafa Kemal talked about projects that amounted to democratic autonomy for the Kurds.

The Kurds were excluded not because Mustafa Kemal made some conscious decision for ethnic cleansing; rather, the British and pro-sultanate forces insisted that Mosul and Kirkuk be left out, despite the National Pact of 1920. Obviously in return for Mosul and Kirkuk, there was an agreement to eliminate the Kurds—similar to what had been done against the Greeks and Armenians. Why did the Republic throw the Kurds out of the system in exchange for concessions from the British Empire? There had been an independence war against this very same British Empire. This is not a historical mistake but a choice consciously made. They thought there was no longer a need for the Kurdish alliance. Besides, there was fear that the British would support the Kurds. The compromise reached was quite similar to the agreements made with the Greeks, the Russians, and the French. Thus in the early years of the Republic, one of the most important antidemocratic steps was taken in respect of the Kurds. The result was tremendous pain that continues today, material losses, and the antidemocratic contraction of the Republic.

The second important antidemocratic step was the deterioration of the alliance with the ummah. There was a constant ideological and daily campaign against the ummah in the name of secularism—the issue was presented as progressive. But in truth, this was the system's hegemonic choice. Putting the ummah and its supporters (the dominant section of society) under its hegemony was a conscious antidemocratic move by the new capitalist modernity. In this connection, the British Empire and other leading European hegemonic powers played important roles. The choice was made with their approval. It was a strategic goal to sever the ties of the Republic of Turkey with the ummah internally and externally.

From the start the system tried to keep representatives of the workers out of the system. This choice resulted not only in the murder of Mustafa Suphi and his friends but in constant prohibitions and arrests.

The bourgeoisie was trying to establish its hegemony under the auspices of the Republic. Taking advantage of its strategic allies, it got permission from capitalist modernity to rule under its own hegemony. The Izmir Economic Congress revealed the Republic's clear preference for capitalism, even as it was just being declared, and also its preference for modernity, through the civil revolutions it initiated. The new state made its preference for Western civilization clear by excluding all its initial allies. Here, instead of Mustafa Kemal's personality, concepts of conjunctural and structural duration prevail. Keeping the declared Republic alive meant alliance with the British Empire. Even though the Republic had a treaty of amity with the Soviet Union, its real friendship had to be with the British.

This truth left its mark on Mustafa Kemal's foreign policy. Mustafa Kemal was a realist: he knew he could keep the Republic alive only through reconciliation with the British Empire, and that's what he did. The Republic's political formation fully complied with British policy. The British gave permission for the Republic to become a nation-state, and in return the Kurds, Islamists, and Socialists were all excluded. The Republic had to reconcile with British policies—it couldn't have ignore its fundamental ally. Especially after the 1930s, the shift toward authoritarian and fascist regimes in line with the then current political situation also influenced the preference for nation-state. The long-term preference of the Republic has clearly been to align itself with Western civilization. Neither a friendly connection with the Soviets nor a return to Islamic religion was ever put back on the agenda.

The Republic's efforts to administer the nation-state through extreme nationalism was considered more important than any democratic step. Contrary to common belief, Mustafa Kemal was not at the forefront of this practice. In 1930 his formation of the new Liberal Republican Party, as well as his profound interest in research on the ancient Sumerians and Hittites, show that he was searching for a patriotism based on Anatolia's cultural wealth and one that would be democratic and not racist. The maintenance of the nation-statist program with all its extremity and rapidity is due to the power of the Union and Progress tradition. Almost no one else fought this tradition. On the contrary, İsmet İnönü, Fevzi Çakmak, Kâzım Karabekir, and most other leading military and civilian bureaucrats had Union and Progress roots and were still its ardent followers. The only difference was that they were now pro-English instead of pro-German. The events after the assassination attempt in Izmir show that Mustafa Kemal was in total isolation. After

1926, he was left amid the bureaucracy and locked in Çankaya[10]. Back then the Zionist movement, affiliated with the British Empire, recommended that Turkey become a homeland for the Jews, up until Israel was established in 1948.

In short, up until the death of Mustafa Kemal [in 1938], the Republic was antidemocratic and hegemonic due to the persistence of the Unionist tradition, with its strict and extreme nation-statist ideology and practice. Despite the priority given to bringing in state capitalism and industrialism, their development was limited. Capitalist modernity, said to be the contemporary Western civilization, could carry out its hegemony only under a one-party authoritarian regime. The democracy problem became extremely aggravated with the emergence of the Democratic Party (DP) between 1945 and 1950. It was also linked with the rise of United States, the new hegemonic power after the Second World War. The DP brought a section of the Islamist gentry into the system. They call this the decline of secularism. In essence, though, the share of the bureaucratic bourgeoisie in state profits has decreased. The fight for profits is fought out in the name of secularism.

The oppressed left also tried to become active in this period; the Kurdish movement had become much weaker. As the three democratic movements oppressed by the Unionist fascism tried to recover, the Republic of Turkey went from being protected by England to being protected by the United States—Turkey joined NATO under U.S. hegemony. The United States ensured such protection through the operations of Gladio, and from 1950 to 2007, all Turkey's military and political structures worked under Gladio's control. In order to grasp the roots of the democratic problem, we must understand that apart from the Jacobin era of 1920-22, Turkey developed under the control of capitalist modernity. Independence is a utopia of the petty-bourgeois: in a world where capitalist modernity is hegemonic, no state or country can be independent. Due to the specific features of Anatolia, the Republic of Turkey is kept within a strict network of dependency.

After the end of the Cold War, the Gladio organization lost its importance, but it continued to be influential in Turkey until 2007 because of the PKK. NATO's Gladio operates under different names in Turkey,

10 The official residence of the president of Turkey.

but whatever it is called, it works against even bourgeois democracy. The Republic of Turkey played an anti-Soviet role from 1920 to 1990, when the USSR collapsed. After the 1990s, there was a plan to use it as a model for the modernization of the Islamic tradition. The existence of the pro-coup and komitadji[11] structures within the state made the Republic of Turkey suitable for such use. It uses this opportunity by playing off of various cliques against one another. The gang warfare within the state worsens the social problems beyond all imagining. It perceives any potential democratic movement as portending its own destruction and thus crushes even the slightest move toward democracy.

The value of the Republic of Turkey to Western civilization is limited to the contribution it makes to the West's security system and to the market and cheap labor it offers to the West's economy. The Republic's struggle with the PKK has revealed this clearly and has proved that the PKK's contradiction is with the system. The objective is not to separate Kurds from Turks. The struggle for democracy in Turkey has revealed the facts about the dominant system and thus has taken on a radical appearance. The PKK's fight is not with the Republic but with the anti-democratism aimed at the Republic. A consistent democratization can break the logjam of nation-statism against nation-statism. The worsening of the democracy problem means that the process of resolving it has begun.

In conclusion, the Oghuz tribes' turn to Islam at the beginning of the eleventh century to resolve their problems marked the beginning of Turkey's democratization problem. The tribal elites tried to become a state, while the poor sections called Turkoman dispersed all over the Middle East in order to maintain their lifeways in a primeval natural democracy. The upper stratum dissolved its ethnic characteristics within the Arabic and Persian cultures, but the Turkoman tribes have preserved their ethnic characteristics to this day. The tribal aristocrats took their place within the main civilization as state rulers and military commanders, whereas the Turkomans participated in partly settled or nomadic lifeways. Mostly, they blended in with the natives. During the Seljuk, Atabeg, and Ottoman eras, the regime developed as the common

11 Armed and underground ultranationalists who will do anything including killing for their state.

civilization of the feudal aristocracy, whereas interrelatedness continued to be the natural way of life for the people.

The ancestors of present-day Turks and Kurds were aware of how critical it was to have strategic relations despite the conflicts between them. Examples of common strategy can be seen as early as the eleventh century. First, the doors to Anatolia were opened for the Oghuz tribes; later, there was a common fight against the Crusader armies. These strategic ties developed on a national basis and went beyond the Turkish and Kurdish principalities. These ties were retained not only in conflicts against the Byzantine Empire and later the Crusaders but also against the Arabic and Persian sultanates, shahdoms, and emirates. The establishment of the Kurdistan Province during the time of the Seljuks demonstrates this fact. This relationship became more striking during the Kurdish Ayyubid Dynasty [1171-1341] and continued its existence during the Artuqid dynasty[12] and the Qara Qoyunlu[13] and Aq Qoyunlu[14] federations. As the Ottoman Empire in expanded toward Iran, Arabia, and the Caucasus, Idris Bitlisi's lengthy diplomatic efforts united the Kurdish principalities, contributing to the Empire doubling in size. The strategic alliance was obvious during this era. In terms of nationality, the Turks and the Kurds were the fundamental nucleus of the empire. These two societies had grown to resemble each other, as a result of natural assimilation and common cultural features. Turkomans with Kurdish roots and Kurds with Turkoman roots multiplied.

At the beginning of the nineteenth century, Napoleon began the infiltration of European modernity into Middle Eastern culture. The occupations and colonialism profoundly upset and transformed the balance of power. Early capitalist modernity in Christian cultures fueled nation-statist tendencies. In the nineteenth and twentieth centuries, modernity through the nation-state tore the millennia-old Middle Eastern culture into pieces and thus led to tremendous chaos and conflict. The nation-state project of Western modernity pulled the Ottoman Empire into

12 An Oghuz Turkish dynasty that ruled in the eleventh and twelfth centuries.

13 Qara Qoyunlu was a Shiite Oghuz Turkic tribal federation that existed from 1378 to 1468.

14 Aq Qoyunlu was a Shiite Oghuz Turkic tribal federation that existed from 1378 to 1508.

pieces. The Committee of Union and Progress tried to establish a parallel state within the state through komitadji but then further aggravated the state crisis by its transition to armed komitadji in 1906. In trying to prevent modernity's nation-state tendencies, they constructed a backward, chauvinistic and fascist nationalism. This Turkish nationalism was put together mostly by people who were not Turkish. This nationalism was the determining factor in the collapse of the empire; the resulting Republican era was difficult and painful and became antidemocratic and ended up in a deadlock.

Although foreign occupation and collaboration with the sultanate increased, between 1919 and 1922 Mustafa Kemal was able, through his Jacobin revolution, to adapt the concept, theory, and institutions of the French Third Republic to Turkey. His chosen model partially resolved the state's crisis, and the Republic of Turkey was established on the ruins of the empire. Although the problem of the state was partially resolved, the social problems became worse. The creation of the Republic, a project of modernity, began when Western hegemonic powers gave their approval in Lausanne [in 1922]. The Jacobin revolution of 1920-22 overcame the state crisis through the establishment of the Republic, but it might have done more. As a result of a still-unclear chain of plots and provocations, it excluded certain secularist Turkish nationalists, socialists, Islamists (with ummah as their political program), and Kurds; had they not been excluded, the Republic might easily have evolved into a democracy. After all, the victory was realized through an alliance of these forces. It is important not to attribute this exclusion and the chain of plots and provocations to Mustafa Kemal—that would not be accurate. Serious plots, assassination attempts, and provocations were made against Mustafa Kemal as well, especially by Unionist cadres that surrounded him. The CHP[15] had a new name, but at heart it was just the renewed form of the Union and Progress Party. In 1930 Mustafa Kemal had tried to break the CHP's monopoly with the Liberal Republican Party but was not successful. After 1935 the CHP's statutes and program were clearly based on the Italian Fascist Party as a model—to which Mustafa Kemal clearly objected.

After 1926, Mustafa Kemal's personal influence did not determine

15 The Republican People's Party.

the Republic's development. The Unionist cadres slowly seized the Republic and tried to institutionalize the fascist mindset on the basis of nation-statism. Mustafa Kemal had a clear policy of keeping the army out of politics, establishing the rule of law, rejecting any class- or community-based guidelines, remaining independent of foreign powers, and pursuing liberationist policies. But the cadres besieging him prevented him from accomplishing these measures, through conspiracies and disbursing of privileges. Such has been the state of affairs to the present day, accomplished through coups. The Unionist coups and conspiracies have all been about seizing the state, continuing despotic governance and turning the state into something that it is not. In return, some very important struggles aimed at maintaining the state according to its true characteristics. Mustafa Kemal's construction of the Republic is a leading example of such efforts.

These two competing streams kept the Turkish state in a continuous crisis throughout the adoption of the Western modernity. It exposed the society to severe problems and prevented the accomplishment of a consistent democracy. The Republic became a profit center for oligarchies, franchises and subversive monopolies and could not free itself of them—it could not become a really secular, democratic, and social state, under the rule of law. The intrastate struggle of these monopolies for hegemony destroyed the social democratic consensus established at the beginning of the 1920s. Their aim was not to establish the rule of law or make the state social, secular, or democratic. Their aim was to reap tremendous profits by acquiring political power.

The history of the Republic can be divided into three phases. The first phase, from 1926 to 1950, was characterized by a one-party authoritarian bureaucratic oligarchy. The second phase, from 1950 to 1980, was characterized by a fierce rivalry between the bureaucratic oligarchy and the landowners, the trade bourgeoisie and the import-substitution industrialists, in order to reallocate state profits. The third phase, from 1980 to 2010, saw the explicit inclusion of global finance capital in state profits as a result of its own direct intervention. The common feature of all three phases is the system established by the state and private capital monopolies, which subjected society and people. Harsh oligarchic methods struggled with state-centered political parties and unions. The hegemonic power that kept the struggle under control was mainly the British Empire from 1925 to 1945 and the United States from 1945 to 2010. After 1950 the Europe, the IMF, and the World Bank were partially included as well. But NATO's Gladio is the real ruler.

The founding allies of the Republic naturally resisted this hegemony. Although they were disorganized and disunited, they resisted throughout all three phases or attempted to integrate into the system. The Soviet Union—and the socialists and communists affiliated with them—were first to be targeted by the hegemonic power. A period of annihilation began with the massacre of Mustafa Suphi[16] and others and with the widespread arrests of members of the Communist Party, and it became more severe with the arrest of Hikmet Kıvılcımlı and Nazım Hikmet. The oppression and arrests increased after 1950, as this made a favorable impression for the impending membership in NATO. The socialists had an opportunity to re-establish themselves with the military coup of May 27, 1960, but they lost it and were suppressed once again with the March 12, 1971, military coup. Much effort was made to continue the resistance, but the 1980 military coup inflicted such a blow that it has never recovered. The representatives of radical democracy are still unable to attain a united and plural organization, and their efforts to continue their existence are disordered, irresponsible, and weak. They still have a duty to act according to their potential and to take steps towards democratization.

Islamists, with ummah as their political program, were subjected to similar blows, widespread arrests, and deportations. They responded with much less resistance, but they did accumulate resentment. The intellectual resistance of Mehmet Akif [Ersoy], Said-i Nursî, and Necip Fazıl [Kısakürek] from 1923 to 1950 was an effort to modernize Islam. In a way, they tried to play the role of Muslim Brotherhood of Turkey, and they reinterpreted Islamic resistance to this end. From 1950 to 1980, they developed relations with the dominant hegemonic powers both within and outside the country and so they became a party to state profits. They thus became part of the monopoly of capital through

16 Mustafa Suphi was a Turkish communist leader who went to Turkey to join the War of Independence. He was murdered, along with other communists, as they set sail on the Black Sea on January 28, 1921.

private capitalism. The Erbakan Movement[17] was a typical Islamic movement of that era. It expressed the longing and interest of many existing movements to take part in political power. aid-i Nursi's movement continued this tendency under the name Nurculuk, with many subbranches and more secretively. All the Islamist movements were influenced by the nineteenth-century Naqshbandi[18] order. They were able to function democratically within themselves, but their democratic stance was neither consistent nor systematic. From 1980 on—first under under Turgut Özal's patronage—until the present they attained political power and became owners of capital but were constantly threatened by the bureaucratic oligarchy. They developed relationships with the United States, Europe, the IMF, the World Bank, and some of the Arabic capitalist circles, which had turned them into partners of the system. After the short-lived prime ministership of ecmettin Erbakan [1996-97] and in the last decade, under ecep Tayyip Erdoğan's leadership, this partnership became more permanent.

These forces face severe problems of democratization. They continually feel that they are under threat from the bureaucratic oligarchy. They must either overcome this threat by making a move to full democratization, or else lose their present position and fracture, much as left-wing movements previously did; the Ergenekon trials [2008] are an expression of such a reality.

The Kurds were an essential and fundamental factor in the founding of the Republic and in the Independence War, yet they now find themselves in the most critical and tragic position before the bureaucratic oligarchy. Indeed, their position is quite bleak, due to many plots, provocations, and banishments. The oligarchy previously implemented ethnic cleansings against Anatolia's Greeks and Armenians. During the Kurdish rebellion period of 1920-38, it attempted to ethnically cleans the region of Kurds. The British Empire played a role similar to the one it played in the elimination of Armenians, Greeks, and Assyrians. Quite early on, the Republic became authoritarian and was made dependent

17 The ideology of Necmettin Erbakan (1926-2011) is set forth in a manifesto entitled Milli Görüs (National View), published in 1969. Erbakan founded an Islamist organization of the same name.

18 Naqshbandi is one of the major spiritual orders of Sufi Islam.

on capitalist modernity. Its relationship with the British Empire was a determining factor. The severe rivalry between the cadres loyal to Mustafa Kemal and those loyal to İsmet İnönü inclined the Republic toward a more right-wing and antidemocratic position. Mustafa Kemal was a friend of the Soviets and had an independent stance, but the other side had a multifaceted relationship with the British Empire.

After the rebellion, the Kurdish question was perceived to have been terminated. The Republic viewed even the slightest movement as a recurrence and immediately crushed it. During the years 1950 to 1980 the Kurds had to try to prove their existence. All discussions and resistance developed around the question "Do the Kurds exist or not?" The PKK emerged to transcend that discussion and enter the process of liberation. From 1980 to 2010, it was objectively the main player, on behalf of all opposition. The problem of democratization became extremely aggravated, especially with the September 12, 1980, military coup. Human rights violations increased around the world, and the state was dominated by gangs. This period ended when the United States withdrew its support from the Ergenekon movement, which then reshaped itself as Turkish Gladio. In November 2007 the United States and the Republic of Turkey concluded an agreement: in return for the elimination of the PKK, the Turkish Gladio would be eliminated. Those who resisted were to be tried, whereas the rest were to be absorbed in the conventional state institutions. Exactly at this point, Turkey witnessed the largest debate on democratization in its republican history and efforts to retransform it into a democratic and constitutional republic.

This biggest of all crises in the history of the Republic, affecting both state and society, continues to date in all its intensity. How we will emerge from it will depend on the attitudes of existing powers. The debate and the quest for a democratic constitution are both the reason for the crisis and its result; in fact, one actively breeds the other. The Kurdish question dominates the agenda yet again. It is a profound historical principle: social problems cannot be forcefully suppressed. Whenever they have a chance, they will make their presence felt more severely than ever before. The period 1920 to 1925 is the most interesting part of history in this respect and is almost being re-lived. The founding allies are being called to rebuild the democratic Republic that could not be built at the time. The fine line between history and the present and the interpretation of the circular progress of events leads us to understand this reality more correctly. It also gives us an opportunity to play our historical roles and creates an opportunity for success.

B — COMING OUT OF THE CRISIS: THE DEMOCRATIC CONSTITUTION

All social parties share an implicit consensus for the democratization of Turkey. What is missing, however, is the transformation of this implicit and historical desire into explicit and live willpower. The democratic constitution is the concise expression of this reality. Part II (above), especially the part on principles, outlines what kind of a democratic constitution is needed in order to fulfill this historical demand for democratization. These principles rest on scientific concept and theory and may be redefined concisely, in order to restructure the Republic on the basis of a democratic constitution which will make it come out of the crisis.

1. Democratic Nation

The democratic nation comprises not only individuals of all cultures, ethnicities, and religions (as well as open and flexible concepts of identity) but also individuals who equally share fundamental rights and freedoms. The democratic nation is based on the principle of the indivisibility of collective and individual rights, in compliance with the undivided common homeland.

2. Common (Democratic) Homeland

The common democratic homeland is the place where citizens of an ecological and democratic society exist as democratic citizens, without specific ethnic or religious trademarks. This definition, with its profound meaning, makes possible the most comprehensive cohesion.

3. Democratic Republic

The democratic republic must base itself on democratic society, as it determines whether the state will be secular, juridical, and social. The ideal form of the state where democracy functions is a republic. In such a republic, secular, social, and juridical features will follow.

4. Democratic Solution

The peaceful coexistence of republican institutions and institutions of democratic society constitute the basis of the democratic solution. The nation-state, monopolies of capitalism, and industrialism must agree to a peaceful coexistence based on reconciliation with the democratic confederalist, economic, and ecological institutions of the democratic society. Frankly, just as it rejects the state with no democracy, there is also no imposition of a democracy without a state.

5. Inseparability of Individual and Collective Rights

Societies are collective just as much as they are individual, and vice versa. To differentiate between them is liberal nonsense, serving exploitation and oppression. Only if individual and collective rights are enjoyed and coherently articulated can such deception be prevented.

6. Ideological Independence and Freedom

In order to democratize soundly and solidly, the ideological hegemony of class civilization and capitalist modernity must be transcended. It is especially difficult to analyze Eastern and Middle Eastern cultures using European positivism and thus attain democratic solutions. Those who can create free concept, theory, and institutions for their own social nature and history might attain such an analysis and solutions and thus achieve freedom.

7. Historicity and Now

Just as history conditions the present, the present substantiates history. But in the present, we have an opportunity to intervene; thus we have a chance to free the present. Just as there is no history without a present, there is no present without a history. The effort of modernity to erase history is an effort to erase the memory, morality, and policies of society and the individual so that people become accustomed to oppression and exploitation and tolerate it. Such dememorization must be totally rejected.

8. Morals and Conscience

Economic and political approaches alone are insufficient to solve social problems and achieve democratization. Society as an entity has always existed, throughout its history, intertwined with morals and conscience. Modernity's war on social morals and conscience aims to legitimize oppression and exploitation. Thus economic and political solutions that stem from this approach can essentially not solve these problems. On the contrary, they will aggravate them and invalidate efforts at democratization. Democratic problem solving allows no room for the principle of power. Instead, there is a need to apply the principles of morals and conscience.

9. Self-Defense of Democracies

Science has shown that not only animate but inanimate entities have a self-defense mechanism at all times and places. Democratic societies, institutions, and individuals must therefore have adequate self-defense against the elements of capitalist modernity—the nation-state, capitalism and industrialism. This is indispensable for a free and equal life.

I believe the short historical evaluation and principles (briefly outlined here) for a democratic constitutional republic will be both informative and analytical as we move toward the democratization of Turkey and solution of the Kurdish issue. It is much easier to situate and analyze the Kurdish question within the question of Turkey's democratic integrity, in order to find a solution model or possible alternatives.

Part IV: THE KURDISH QUESTION AND THE PROSPECTS FOR ITS SOLUTION

Perhaps the very first social problem, which began with the onset of class civilization, relates to the origins of the Kurds. The Kurti, Hurrian, Gutian, and Aryan[19] concepts from early Sumerian civilization all mean "mountain people," a name still used today for present-day Kurds. The Sumerian civilization, which developed as an antithesis to Neolithic society, denotes the emergence of Upper Mesopotamia as an alternative to Lower Mesopotamia. The problems of Neolithic society were linked to this emergence. Of course, it would not be scientific to assert that Neolithic society is identical to present-day Kurdishness. But the similarities between the continuing heritage of the Neolithic society and the society of 10,000 years ago can be no coincidence. Social history suggests the links between them must have been firm; archaeology and etymology say that similarities are much stronger. The society at the skirts of the Zagros and Taurus mountain ranges may well have had proto-Kurdish features.

In antiquity (the period from 5000 B.C. to the expansion of Islam), basic institutions of civilization grew rapidly: hierarchy, dynasty, state, town, trade, agriculture, craft, family, woman, slavery, religion, inscription, science, literature, sculpture, architecture, and industrial production. Social problems grew rapidly as well, and Proto-Kurds are at the center of these problems. Their solution was to focus on agriculture and animal husbandry and to take refuge in mountain peaks to escape their enemies—features still fundamental to present-day Kurds. The ruling hierarchy of the Proto-Kurds resolved their own class and social problems by fusing with nearby state civilizations. The remaining laborer communities, like the nomadic tribes and clan, struggled to survive in the battle for existence, living at times in the mountains and at other

19 See prison writings volume I

times in the plains. The Kurds resorted to the mountains and worked with agriculture and animal husbandry, while present-day Armenians and Assyrians took up the crafts and trades of the towns. It was as if there was a natural division of labor. The main peoples of the Tigris and Euphrates were interlinked with this dialectic of life.

Christianity brought these people their first big separation. The conceptual god of Abraham, Jehovah, had previously represented a more profound division. New social problems created by the growing complexity and intensity of civilization expressed themselves in the form of new gods and religions. As social problems grew and diversified, concepts of god and religion became more complex. The Zoroastrian religion, around the Zagros Mountains, denoted the sublimity—that is, the divinity—of agriculture and animal husbandry, whereas the gods of Sumeria, Babylonia, Akkadia, and Assyria reflected town, trade, state, and dynasty. Christianity was initially a religion of the oppressed and poor, denoting yet another quest for a solution to social problems through god's religion and manner. Judaism was born as a tribal religion, but Christianity arose from it as the religion of the people. It was the first huge step toward ummah and ecumenism. Islam, in its early days, based itself on the people and ummah; during the time of its rule, however, it became hegemonic as the civilizational religion of the dominant class and the state.

From the birth of Islam (in the 7th century) until the entrance of capitalist modernity into the Middle East in the 1800s, medieval Kurdishness continued to live according to the heritage of Antiquity. The upper stratum—emirates, principalities, chiefs, and sheikhs—integrated with the dominant civilization, be it Arabs, Persian, or Turkish. They abandoned Kurdish lifeways, as it was not in their interest to be Kurdish—their interests pressured them to become good Arabs, Persians and Turks. And thus the social problem became more complex for the Kurds, not only because it was the oppressed identity but also because it was the betrayed cultural identity.

Would the problems of the Kurds have been resolved if they had become a state? During the period of real socialism, it was believed that they would have. It was thought that if peoples and/or identities formed their own state, then all their problems would be solved once and for all. This should not surprise us—even socialism sought to establish a proletarian state. And Kurds deplored the fact that we never had a state. But democratic civilization now proves to us that the state is the greatest source of troubles. There is no such thing as the state of Arabs, Persians or Turks. These are illusions of the nation-state created only recently, in the last hundred years! Islam had a common state. Although they sometimes quarreled because of their interests, their dominant hükemas[20] were united. Islam also had a people and ummah. But then their worlds diverged, and this problem eventually became worse. Just as the problems were common, so were the solutions. They tried to express their problems in the name of religion and god and to resolve them in this manner. Kurdishness, Arabness, Persianness, and Turkishness existed as a cultures, and their problems were expressed in terms of religion. Neither the Umayyad Dynasty nor the Abbasids were the state of Arabs alone; similarly, the Seljuks and the Ottoman states were not exclusive to Turks. The Persian tradition of establishing states was not based on any particular race. The upper stratum of any ethnicity strengthens its existence by becoming a state, throwing their ethnic fellows into a whirl of social problems: examples are the Kurds, Armenians, Assyrians, Greeks, Turkomans, Bedouins, and stateless Persians.

Capitalist modernity entered the Middle East with its nation-state, capitalism, and industrialism. For the cultural identities and peoples robbed of their values, it meant near death. These people, who had previously been betrayed by the wise men and hükemas of the upper stratum, were now hunted by capitalist modernity. Starting at the beginning of the nineteenth century, they were made to fight one another in the name of nation-statism. In addition, they were made to work under terrible conditions in the workplaces of capitalism and industrialism. They were turned into tools for profits and capital. Alienation was thus spread over three eras: Antiquity, the Middle Ages, and Modern Times.

As nationalism was imposed on all cultures, the Kurds had their share of disasters, indeed experienced it most severely. Their nation-statism did not result in victory. The upper stratum, befitting its heritage, took its place within the neighboring nation-states and deemed the traditional culture worthy of betrayal. They competed to prove themselves

20 Muslim philosophers who islamized Greek philosophy.

the best Arabs, Persians, or Turks. The more they betrayed their cultural values and identities, the more profits, money, and salaries they could have. Kurdishness, for its part, thought it could protect itself by taking refuge in the sacred lifeways of proto-Kurds; agriculture, animal husbandry, and mountains.

A—THE HISTORICAL DIALECTIC IN THE RELATIONSHIP BETWEEN THE TURKS AND KURDS

A more concrete and close-up evaluation of the Turkish-Kurdish dilemma may clarify the problems. Amid the merciless whirl of the use of force, neither the problems nor their solutions can be adequately understood. But if enlightenment and consciousness are close to the truth, then half of the solution is already attained. The other half is to take the appropriate steps in the path that has been paved.

[In the eleventh century,] when the Seljuks, both as a tribe and as a principality, arrived at the borders of Kurdistan (which was when Seljuk sultans probably first coined the name Kurdistan), they proposed that the Kurds join them in a common war against the Byzantines, and they employed the instrument of Islamic brotherhood to convince them. The Kurds supported the common war strategy, since the overwhelming majority of them had already adopted Islam and since they had experienced frequent setbacks against the Byzantines. In May 1071, Sultan Alp Arslan tried to secure an alliance with the Kurdish principalities and tribes in Meyafarqîn (present-day Silvan), then the capital of the Kurds. In August 1071, with forces composed of fighters both from principalities and tribes, he achieved a momentous victory. Approximately half the fighters were Kurds. For the Turkish tribes and principalities, the victory was strategic—it opened the door to Anatolia. For the Kurdish tribes and principalities, it removed the Byzantine threat. The relationship between Turks and Kurds had been given an important basis.

Subsequently Turkish tribes and principalities focused more on Anatolia, which opened up Central Anatolia and the routes to the Western Mediterranean and the Black Sea. The Kurdish tribes and principalities, meanwhile, continued to develop their own areas of settlement and power. The Turkish tribes and principalities never tried to seize or appropriate the Kurdish-dominant areas or cultural traditions. The strategic alliance, solidarity, and common culture that they shared demanded this approach. The Armenian and Assyrian peoples too continued to live in friendship, mostly in the cities. There were denominational differences between them and the Byzantines, so their withdrawal from the region did not affect them negatively.

During the Islamic era, some Turkish principalities, such as the Artuqids, Qara Qoyunlus, and Aq Qoyunlus, established themselves in Kurdistan, but they mostly disappeared into the Kurdish culture through natural assimilation. Traces can still be seen today. The Kurds, on the other hand, continued to live under numerous local principalities as well as tribes and clans—but their problems worsened. Their features as a people developed, but as with the Turkish tribes, their upper stratum advanced their principalities by serving the numerous civilizations. In the meantime, the lower strata, the Kurmanj (Kurdmanj) diverged into a separate category. This divergence paralleled that of Arab-Bedouin and Turk-Turkoman, and it accelerated among the Kurds. Up until the onset of the Ottoman reign (early 1500s), Turkish and Kurdish principalities and tribes exhibited an implicit respect for each other's jurisdiction. They also, more often than not, acted according to a common strategy when both faced external threats. Positive relations outweighed clashes, and no systematic contradiction could be observed among them.

The second important strategic stage in Kurdish-Turkish relations began when the Ottoman Empire expanded into the Middle East. At the beginning of the sixteenth century, the tension between the Safavid Dynasty (based on Shi'a, in Iran) and the Kurdish principalities grew due to conflicts based on denominational differences. In fact, the tension was exacerbated all over Anatolia. Similarly, the Mamluk sultans of Egypt increased their influence in the Mediterranean and the Southeast, creating similar tensions. The Kurdish principalities held a strategic position, and whoever they align themselves with would become the hegemonic power of the Middle East.

The strategic alliance established by the Ottoman sultan Selim I between two almost equal powers was historic. It acknowledged a wide autonomy and governmental authority for the Kurdish principalities. Going well beyond an alliance, it paved the way for a Turkish-Kurdish empire, similar to the Austrian-Hungarian Empire. Another historical example is the strategic partnership among Hittites, Hurrians, and Mitannis as early as 2000 B.C. during their initial civilizational attempt. They depended on one another, and economic and political relations rapidly integrated them. This historical phenomenon manifested itself once again during the Ottomans' magnificent century.

Their new status increased the significance of the Sunni Kurdish principalities within the Empire. But the situation of the Alevi and Yazidi Kurds worsened, and the problems experienced by the Kurmanj became more severe. Contradictions based on class and denomination also became more pronounced. This partnership lasted approximately three hundred years but deteriorated as capitalist modernity crept into the Middle East. The British Empire increased its influence in the region through Iraq and Egypt and tried to develop a nationalism centered on Sulaymaniyah. Baban tribal leaders from the Sulaymaniyah region mounted an initial uprising. The Kurdish situation has undergone continuous change for approximately two hundred years, continuing to date in the form of a half nation-state in South Kurdistan [Iraq]. The nineteenth-century Kurdish rebellions are protocapitalist-nationalist because of their class attributes. All the other nationalities that composed the empire separated and established their own nation-states, but for historical reasons the Kurds did not separate from the Turks. The state nucleus of the empire had a mentality based on the two-nation partnership of the upper stratum. For strategic reasons, all civilizations that emerged in these two areas since the birth of state had to act together; otherwise the existence and interests of these societies would have been under threat. The value of being in partnership is clear from the emerging political and economic development.

The ventures of the Seljuk and Ottoman sultans once again verify this historical dialectic. The partnership between prince and sultan right at the top in time turned into a relationship among sheikh, agha, and merchant. It deteriorated further with Mahmud II (1808-1839), increasing the conflict between the two sides and producing a century of rebellion.

The inconclusiveness of the rebellions and efforts to reconstruct the Ottoman Empire in a nation-statist manner destroyed the traditional relationship between the two nations. When the Young Ottomans, Young Turks, and finally the most nationalist of them all, the Committee of Union and Progress (1889) began to first covertly and then openly defend Turkish nation-statism, the gap between them increased.

In the face of such developments, Kurdish nationalism began to manifest itself. The appearance of the Kurdish question in modern times coincides with this period. When the Committee of Union and Progress began forming komitadji and turned to Turkism instead of Islamic nationalism, the existing problems became more severe. There were now two sections: Turkish nationalism based on race, and Islamic nationalism. The Kurds tried to continue their traditional unity with the Islamic nationalists. The sheikhs of the Naqshbandi order, Mawlana Khalid and Said Nursi, both represented that mainstream tendency, insisting on a common empire and later a common state formation. The ideology of Islam and ummah were being modernized to this end. In the aftermath of the princedoms (1878) the sheikhs and religious orders, whose influence and social leadership role increased, continued with such an arrangement to the present.

The Committee for Union and Progress, on the other hand, especially after its defeat in the Balkan Wars (1912-13), turned to a racist nationalism within the state, disregarding the historical partnership between Anatolia and Mesopotamia. Their nationalism had no room for Kurdishness. Like the Armenians, the Kurds would either have to leave their own land or, in one way or another, be eradicated. French positivism fostered this policy. Only the strong had the right to life; there was an effort to implement Darwin' s "survival of the fittest" in society. The brutality of capitalist modernity appeared here in all its horror. This strict positivist ideology made life uninhabitable not only for Armenians, Greeks, Assyrians, and Kurds but also for Turks and Arabs—it was terminated by the Committee for Union and Progress as the empire came to an end. But during Republican Turkey, its influence remained dominant. (A discussion of the Jacobin character of the Republican revolution, of its alliances, and of the leadership of Mustafa Kemal can be found in the preceding section and will not be repeated here.) The

Kurds were co-founders of the Republic, taking their place, as they had done throughout history, both within the pro-ummah liberation and in the construction of the Republic as a strategic partner.

When the British Empire gave them nation-state privileges within the borders set up by the National Pact, in return for Mosul and Kirkuk, the division of the Kurds into four parts began. At the same time policies to terminate the existence of the remaining Kurds within these borders took off rapidly and mercilessly; this policy has continued at the same speed ever since. I must add that the Treaty of Zuhab[21] signed with the Iranian Safavid dynasty in 1639 violated the strategic alliance between the two nations. Almost all the Kurds were within the borders of the Ottoman Empire. The National Pact border was definitely constructed on the basis of Kurdish and Turkish unity. The agreements made with the English and French were most certainly against the National Pact, as these agreements made the existence or nonexistence of the Kurds an issue, more severe than ever before in their history. It most definitely contradicted the often-mentioned thousand-year-old partnership and fraternity between Turks and Kurds. The question not asked, however, is who was responsible for these agreements. On the one hand, you divide the Kurds into four parts in return for the concessions received as a result of agreements with some of the hegemonic powers—on the other hand, you scream and shout that "some Kurds are destroying the thousand-year-old fraternity!" This approach, which ignores facts, has brought the Kurdish question to the brink of cultural genocide throughout the Republic's history.

The implementations that denied the spirit of the thousand-year-old strategic friendship caused the Kurdish question to become more than an economic, social, political and military issue. It became an issue of the cultural existence of a people. The rebellions (1925-40) were the result of this problem of existence but were also employed to that end. The Unionist mentality quite clearly wanted to push the Kurds out of both state and society and even stop their existence as a society. Hence the longtime policy question: "Do the Kurds exist or not?" Try to

21 This accord was signed between Safavid and Ottoman Empires on 17 May 1639 over territorial disputes, dividing the Kurdish inhabited areas between them. Today's border between Iran and Turkey mostly follows that agreement.

understand how horrific it is to pass from being regarded as cofounder of the Republic to being subjected to a process of extermination. For Kurds, the question is not separation but overcoming the process of extermination and once again attaining the historic position of strategic friend, partner, and confrère. This reality can only be grasped with true empathy.

B—THE REPUBLIC'S CAPITALIST MODERNITY PROJECT AND EMERGENCE OF THE PKK

The forces that constructed the Republic represented a democratic reconciliation. Mustafa Kemal's leadership was both the reason and result of this reconciliation. The 1921 Constitution and the first Grand National Assembly of Turkey show the nature of this reconciliation quite clearly. It was often mentioned that the Turks and the Kurds were the two fundamental components of the ummah, together with anti-imperialism and friendship with the Soviets. Examples are abundant in the assembly records. To be a socialist, to be a Kurd, or to be from Kurdistan was regarded as entirely natural. Clearly the Jacobin period of the Republic reflected the general consensus of the society. At the time, the British Empire was the main target.

But when the revolution terminated the occupation and a new order was to be constructed, things changed. Unionist cadres (those who were pro-British) tried to neutralize Mustafa Kemal; their numerous plots and provocations, including the Sheikh Said provocation and a direct assassination attempt, bore fruit from 1925 onward. This group became stronger during the prime ministership of İsmet İnönü. Mustafa Kemal eliminated İnönü just before his death, but the end result was unchanged.

After the Second World War, world hegemony passed to the United States, which offered further help for this group. Although İsmet İnönü tried to appear impartial, he was close to this group. As a matter of fact, it was not the Democratic Party leadership but İsmet İnönü himself who established strategic relations with the United States. In 1944, before Turkey even became a member of NATO, the first group of Turkish military officers went to the United States for training. Relations between the two countries intensified during the term of the Democratic Party. In 1952 NATO's Gladio, directly under the leadership of the United States, was established within the army. In Turkey, Gladio first organized itself as the Mobilization Inspection Board, whose budget and administration was provided by the United States. Thereafter it expanded and extended itself into economic, social, political, military, and cultural areas. It controlled all the legal political parties, and it kept the working class under its control through the Türk-İş[22], established in 1952. Gladio applied relentless pressure on the Communist Party and unions aligned with the Soviets. Its chief goal was to crush even the slightest Communist or Socialist infiltration. Insofar as Kurdishness was associated with these leftist groups, it subjected Kurdishness to this treatment. It established strategic and secret relations with newly established Israel and developed relations with traditional religious and primitive nationalist families and individuals within the Kurdish community. It established ties with the Iranian and Iraqi monarchies. The Central Treaty Organization (CENTO) was the umbrella organization for these relationships. The overall aim was to prevent the spread of communism into the Middle East.

Clearly this model, developed under U.S. leadership, was the new vision of capitalist modernity in the Cold War of the 1950s. The Republic of Turkey played a leading role in establishing the renewed modernity of the United States, both in its own country and in the Middle East. The modernity propounded by Mustafa Kemal was different: it was more like the Soviet version and rested on strategic friendship with the Soviet Union. To correctly analyze the modernity of the 1950s and even that after 1925 (despite Mustafa Kemal), one must see the differences between the two modernities. In their implementation of nation-statism, capitalism, and industrialism, they have serious class, political, diplomatic and economic differences. Ultimately, first the British Empire and then the United States won the hegemonic war. Besides, those two have always had strategic ties. The modernity they applied not only eliminated democratic reconciliation within the Republic but, by declaring a war against them all, turned fundamental allies into enemies.

22 The Confederation of Turkish Trade Unions

What Mustafa Kemal found hard to understand is exactly this point. The fact that he was under the profound influence of positivist ideology contributed to this. His passion for independence and freedom and his respect for the local Anatolian culture confined the destructive effect of positivism, but could not prevent its influence.

Positivist dogmatism was substituted for religious dogmatism and still has a profound influence on the secular-nationalists in Turkey. Contrary to widespread belief, this secularism is not about democratic republicanism—it is not even republican. It is despotic and dictatorial. Unionism is typical, and the Republican People's Party (CHP) represents what it could have influenced. Carl Schmitt's thesis on the religious and political theology of 1920s and 1930s Germany is more suitable for the philosophy of law and politics in Turkey. All the political concepts of modernity can be found in medieval theology. I think it has Sumerian origins. The only thing positivism has done is to polish them, present them as "scientific," and propagate them in the name of capitalism. Mustafa Kemal's doubts and hesitations, his intensely agitated moods, and his lengthy readings on various civilizations shows that he had some differences and similarities with positivist and religious dogmatism.

When it comes to modernity all the elitist cadres of the Republic of Turkey share a profound ignorance and disbelief intertwined with dogmatism. They all do, whether they are right wing or left wing, secular or religious, Alevi or Sunni, Turkish or Kurdish. Between the elements of capitalist modernity and pro-ummah Islamists, socialists, Kurdish nationalist, and even some Turkish nationalists conflicts developed. It has not yet been analyzed how these conflicts were prompted and channeled. The manipulation by the U.S. Gladio had disastrous consequences. The relationship between the elements of capitalist modernity and the komitadj and subversive perceptions and organizations within the state for the past one hundred years must be exposed. If it is not, then neither the state nor the social crisis nor the tension and conflict between them can be understood. The relationship of the system to the hegemonic powers, especially Britain and United States, must be exposed because it has a vital effect on democratization and on the solution of the Kurdish question. All efforts for independence and freedom by Mustafa Kemal and those devoted to him remained idle, with adverse results; to understand why, one must understand what happened with the Republic's modernity project. We may understand which internal and external forces were influential, and the ideological hegemony upon which they depended, by analyzing their economic, social, political, and military practices. Military coups and their civil extensions were never able to overcome their dependence on the cause-and-effect spiral of these contradictions and conflicts. Social scientists agree that all their efforts to rescue things only aggravated the problems and created deadlock. The Republic's modernity project was crippled from the very start. This disability must be mentioned repeatedly because it is what moved the Republic into conflict with the all fundamental elements of power that liberated the country and established the Republic. This inherent disability can be seen by just looking at the dates of the mentioned conflicts: 1925-26, 1930, 1937-38[23], 1945-50, 1960, 1971, 1980[24], 1997[25], and 2001-2002[26].

The founders of the Republic reasserted their presence during the period 1965-80, but they did not analyze or sufficiently understand the traditional hegemonic bloc of power and oligarchy—they embarked on a quest to secure their own existence. Contrary to their claims, they were unprepared in any way to accomplish a revolution or a counter-revolution—yet that was how they were portrayed. The moment they rebelled, they were partially crushed, and the remaining structures were infiltrated in order to tame them. Unfortunately, the force used against one another was far removed from understanding the role of Gladio. During this period, the link between nationalist and Islamist organizations and the anti-Communist Gladio tactics are much more apparent. The impact of these forces on economic and cultural life was also important. What determined all of social life was the members of senior administration of the institutions of capitalist modernity who sided with Gladio. Gaining control over the army and the political structures was the first priority. This use of Republican administration was clearly in the style of Union and Progress komitadj. The efforts of Mustafa Kemal

23 1925-26 Sheikh Said uprising, 1930 Ararat rebellion, 1937-38 massacres in Dêrsim
24 Military coup d'états in 1960, 1971 and 1980
25 "post-modern military coup"
26 severe economic and state crisis

Atatürk were not sufficient to counter it. If Republic could not overcome the komitadj and the subversive (in terms of coups) tradition as well as the control exercised by Gladio, then its democratic and juridical features as well as its order and stability could not be ensured.

Thus we see that the problematic structure of the Republic played a determining role in the emergence of the PKK. In the 1970s the movement toward democracy gained strength. The March 12 coup d'état could not stop the process. The social forces that had been influential in the establishment of the Republic reappeared. Socialism, Islamism, and Kurdish nationalism sought legitimacy within the Republic. If their many democratic demands had not been suppressed through coups and fascist implementations, a solution through democratization would have been attained. But instead increasingly repressive and fascistic methods were employed to overcome the crisis of the cold war and elements of modernity. The Republic of Turkey was the country where Gladio's control was the most severe; the September 12 regime was the most striking example of this control.

The PKK could not be totally suppressed because of the internal structure of the Kurdish and the Middle Eastern upheavals. Indeed, the September 12 [1980] coup d'état almost calmed everything down within twenty-four hours, but when it came to the Kurds, there was a more profound reason for the rulers' delusion: belief was widespread that the Kurds, both as a society and as a people, had been terminated. After the Kurdish rebellions were crushed, a brutal period of assimilation followed. It looked as if the Kurds could never possibly recover. The new bureaucracy, the middle class, and the mentality of capitalist modernity considered them to be wiped out, and their role in history was forgotten. Their frail and odd existence was regarded as primitive. The Kurdish upper strata continued to masterfully play their role as the servants to the rulers. The nationalists and those devoted to a particular sect, especially those associated with the United States, kept themselves at a distance and would have nothing to do with the resistance and freedom struggle. The PKK developed relations with the poor peasant and urban dwellers of the Kurmanj section of the Kurdish society, although they too were devastated under these conditions. The PKK not only benefited from but rekindled patriotism and Kurdishness—it re-created cultural structures. The Kurdish people's social nature, despite being overwhelmed and divided, contained structuralities. The only thing needed was a minimal patriotism and some conceptual knowledge. These enchanting emotions and concepts had already been sufficiently formed in the PKK. The PKK needed no high-ranking diplomatic or political cadres; it needed only a rapid mobilization of these emotions and concepts. The limited actions that had been taken provided the required momentum.

So it developed itself from its first emergence in the 1970s to the beginning of 1980. The September 12 regime used excessive force and suppressed the other left wing and opposition forces. Combined with this was the reality of Diyarbakır Prison and our deployment in the Middle East, and so it would only be a matter of time before the armed struggle, called the period of August 15, 1984, would begin. The period could have been initiated in 1982, but some of those in the mountains had not accomplished their tasks properly, so the move had to be postponed to 1984. The war between Iran and Iraq also contributed to this already suitable framework. But the movement was never completely abolished from Kurdistan within Turkey's borders; it always protected its existence there. The PKK had not yet become professional guerrillas; they were more like bad copies. The state had not expected the action taken on August 15. But we did not even properly exploit the advantages of this. The deployment in the Middle East was enough to maintain the movement and attain the support of all parts of Kurdistan and of the Kurds in Europe, despite the opposition of numerous forces in Iraqi Kurdistan.

The September 12 regime's intervention began to produce favorable results, and so with the support of NATO, it made the transition to a State of Emergency. JITEM[27] was also formed at about this time. The NATO Gladio, under the leadership of Germany, had effectively come into play since 1985. Conspiracies against the pope and Olof Palme[28]

27 The intelligence service of the gendarmerie, responsible for many of the worst human rights violations.

28 On May 13, 1981, at Vatican City, Mehmet Ali Ağca, a known fascist assassin from Turkey, attempted to assassinate John Paul II. The assassination of Olof Palme, the prime minister of Sweden, took place on February 28, 1986, in Stockholm, a crime unresolved today. Both episodes were used to criminalize PKK.

can be evaluated by fitting them into the more general plans of the system; directly and indirectly they were part of the attempt to foil the positive effects of the emergence of guerrillas in Kurdistan. For the PKK, the armed struggle played a secondary role from 1973 to 1983—ideology and politics were more prominent back then. The action of 1984 was primarily military, but the PKK also continued to improve itself ideologically and politically.

The role played by the State of Emergency and JITEM needs to be specifically and profoundly analyzed. It is well known that many degenerate acts were conducted within and outside the movement. Among these were actions that had no consideration for the presence of women and children, the targeting of sections that should not have been targeted, the tendency to extreme arbitrariness, and the negligence of even the minimum required tasks.

But the more they demonized the PKK, the more it gained strength. This indicates the profound need felt by the Kurdish people. The number of Kurds affected by the policies of forced migration are greater than the number of displaced Armenians, Greeks, and Assyrians. All this, however, positively influenced the relationship between PKK and the Kurdish people. Historical and geographical conditions were also significant. The fundamental factor was that the development corresponded to the historical desire to protect existence and human dignity. The spontaneity of historical demands should not be belittled.

President Turgut Özal's policy in 1992 in relation to the Kurds was unexpected, and we realized its importance a little too late. I always consider it a historical loss that with his death we lost a serious opportunity to resolve the issue. The Republic could have had an opportunity for a democratic resolution, although some people within Gladio probably had no intention of allowing this. The then chief of staff, Doğan Güreş, stated, as he arrived from England at the beginning of 1990: "They gave me the go-ahead for elimination." Fundamental issues that still require clarification include the Tansu Çiller coup after Turgut Özal's death and the consecutive plots put into action within and outside the army. It has been documented that Tansu Çiller was an agent of the CIA. This partially explains what happened. I think the killing of many real Kemalist intellectuals and prominent Kurdish people, the thousands of murders with unknown offenders, the evacuations of thousands of villages, and the revival of Hezbollah constitute one of the biggest plots against the Republic. It reminds me of the conspiratory and rebellious 1924-27 period, during Mustafa Kemal's term. Back then the democratic elements that were part of the foundation of the Republic were eliminated too. This situation is far from being resolved, even today. But the winners are clearly the British Empire and capitalist modernity. We must also not underestimate the role of the international hegemony and its stringent collaborators in aborting the chance for a democratic solution at the beginning of the 1990s through similar plots, rebellions, and murders. The chaos, massacres, provocations, and the forced demographic movements committed from 1993 to 1997 are the best examples of what the hegemonic control over the Republic actually meant.

We are talking about a period where the juridical, secular, social and democratic functions of the state were totally eliminated, and placed under the control of JITEM, and all the monopolistic structures within the elements of capitalist modernity were rushed to their service. This was a rare but interesting time. Toward the end of this era, Prime Minister Necmettin Erbakan through the president of Syria and a section of the army in the name of the Social Relations Department via Brussels tried to get in touch with us. We responded positively; letters and information were exchanged. But this attempt was unsuccessful, as Necmettin Erbakan was removed from his position, and I was forced to leave the Middle East. I am of the opinion that the role of the internal and international Gladio circles in this failure should not be underestimated. The huge crisis, conflict, and the low-intensity warfare that the Republic is still going through could have been prevented. Both the unilateral ceasefire and the relationship with the Erbakan government created another opportunity. These attempts were suppressed and the opportunity was intentionally wasted.

My later arrival in Europe and attempt to find a political solution was clearly annulled by Britain. I was kidnapped on British orders and taken to Kenya in a private jet that took off from Switzerland; Britain was in collaboration with the Gladio administration in Athens. Of course all European members of NATO were involved in the operation, but Britain was the mastermind. The United States was the official operator, while Israel was guiding the operation and was the force that prevented me from staying in Moscow. Long ago, while I was in Kenya and the Middle East, the Israelis had told me to seek refuge with them, but I did not trust them and never thought of trusting them. They were trying to scuttle the Kurds' prospect for freedom by targeting me personally. I was quite sure that no one, including myself, could dare or think of something like this. Interestingly, tactics used against the Republican administration

were now being tried on me and, via the PKK, on the Kurds as well. Elements of capitalist modernity, so profoundly connected with one another, had stepped in again.

I was calm and patient after learning my lesson from what had happened at İmralı. I preserved my stance during the interrogation, trial, and arrest. I believe the interrogators employed tactics that changed daily. They incorrectly interpreted my calmness and patience; similar incorrect interpretations were made within and outside the organization. But despite all these wrong interpretations, I never deviated from my stance. I am now in the eleventh year of my incarceration, and I have gone through a four-layered period of defense.

The First Defense Layer: During the trial, I tried to give my opinion in a small booklet called Demokratik Çözüm Manifestosu.[29] It might have been not all that well prepared, but it presented the cornerstones for a democratic solution. It is a pity that government and others in political circles did not make use of it. The process was just left, and they all believed that it would somehow be resolved. Some pro-solution steps taken by the then Prime Minister Bülent Ecevit were wasted by his coalition partner, MHP. The AKP was not even interested in a definition of the problem. It may have found the "road map", drawn up long ago, indexed to North Iraq (South Kurdistan), sufficient. I never received responses to the letters I wrote to the senior officials, Mr. Abdullah Gül and Mr. Recep Tayyip Erdoğan, in their official capacities, and the defense I prepared on my own behalf against the eleven cell-confinement penalties[30] issued against me. Up until 2005 time was wasted. Thus a

29 It appeared in English as *Declaration on the Democratic Solution of the Kurdish Question*

30 During these penalties, the author was deprived of even the limited rights he could enjoy in his cell. Since he was the only prisoner on the island, he was never placed in

new period of action was inevitable.

The Second Defense Layer: The defense I prepared here at the İmralı Island Prison entitled Sümer Rahip Devletinden Halk Cumhuriyetine Doğru[31] was presented to the European Court of Human Rights as two books. It was a more profound attempt at detailing the democratic solution.

The Third Defense Layer: My defense entitled Bir Halkı Savunmak[32] was taken up at the Grand Chamber of the European Court of Human Rights. It constituted the third layer. The formation of the Kurdish question and prospects for a solution were further crystallized.

The Fourth Defense Layer: The process I am currently in is the fourth and final defense layer. I completed four of the five volumes that have been named in general as Demokratik Toplum Manifestosu.[33] The volumes in succession have been named the following: (1) Uygarlik, (2) Kapitalist Uygarlik, (3) Özgürlük Sosyolojisi, (4) Ortadogu'da Uygarlik Krizi ve Demokratik Uygarlik Çözümü, and (5) Türkiye ve Kürdistan'da Demokratik Uygarlık Çözümü. The fifth volume will be completed in the future[34]. This Road Map is a rough framework of the fifth volume.

The armed struggle of the last twenty-five years (1984-2009) may be identified as the fight for truth. It refers to the revelation of facts, not to the liberation of a society. Around the world, historical and social problems can be resolved only when facts about them are revealed. Besides, military victories constitute a continuous source of problems unless they are mandatory, legitimate wars of self-defense. What is important about this twenty-five-year war is not whether there was a victory or a defeat but whether it resolved the problem. What did the Hundred Years' War between England and France achieve, other than to prove that the Channel is the border? The last quarter-century has been decisive in proving the existence of the Kurds. At first it was the PKK's goal to

---

a different cell during the execution of the penalty. The defense mentioned here was never given to his defense team.

31 Prison Writings, vol. 1, The Roots of Civilization, and vol. 2, The PKK and the Kurdish Question in the 21st Century

32 In translation process, working title: "In Defence of a People"

33 All these volumes are currently being translated.

34 This volume has now been completed and handed to the authorities to be sent to the European Court of Human Rights. It reached the Court in March 2011.

crown the Kurdish people's existence with a nation-state. But toward the end of this period, we saw that this crown was not all that necessary. On the contrary, it is the source of many new problems, as we have seen and learned from many examples. Instead, a democratic formation of society will be more meaningful.

Understanding its development is the best way to correctly understand the PKK. In the 1970s, against the background of the cold war, the PKK thought it should be counted in the real-socialist camp. The positions it took reflected this intention. Intellectually the PKK did not really go beyond revolutionary emotions and concepts. Back then, revolutionary willpower was much more significant; it was the ideal of free living that inspired us, not ideology. So we were not seriously affected when real socialism was no longer favored. It was a movement based on morality and belief more than a modernist left-wing party. Yes, it had theory, but the essential binding values were morality and belief. Perhaps the most important asset of Kurdish society, during the period of war and to date, is the difficult conditions of life that have determined its strength, courage, and the enduring morality. This may be one of the main reasons why it is more productive and advanced. None of the splits and losses the PKK experienced impeded its development. Most important, it did not get carried away with the modernist left-wing party and lifestyle. The PKK underwent a profound social struggle within itself because of its contradictory social reality and the strength it obtained from freeing itself from this social reality. This internal struggle, which a modernist party could not have survived, also contributed to the PKK's sound development.

The real transformation in PKK occurred when it abandoned its goal to establish a state, and its state-centered approach in general, and adopted the course toward democratic political formations. The reason for the change of direction was not the difficulties involved in establishing a real socialist nation-state. The real reason was the real-socialist lifestyle; it was no different from capitalist life across the world. The PKK would either find a way to live in a different world or it would dissolve, just as real socialism did.

Because I had time in İmralı, I could give more attention to the democratic solution and to construct it profoundly. Before my incarceration,

I had limited time to focus on it. My defenses and prior dialogues strikingly reflect the depth of this path. Neither the state nor the PKK could grasp this development for a long time; they considered it a mere tactical approach. Some thought it was the beginning of some sort of an elimination process, when in fact a great depth in political theory and sociological enlightenment had been reached. The PKK underwent a comprehensive transformation. Those who acted irresponsibly and thus immorally used this moment of transition as an excuse to abandon it. The decisive factor in the departures after 2000 was the moral weaknesses experienced before the seriousness of the transformation.

The state and relevant left-wing circles were expecting the PKK to self-destruct. This expectation was not only wrong but irresponsible. If the state had acted more responsibly, then after 1999 there would have been historical democratic transformations. A historical opportunity was truly wasted when the state did not adequately respond to our one-sided efforts. The disintegration of the left saw it end up in liberal individualism. Its approach was much more irresponsible than the state's. Those who abandoned us respected no moral boundaries. Once again, though unexpectedly, it became quite clear that Kurdish communities cannot be deceived for long. The pain we suffered had taught us incredible lessons. An average show of loyalty was enough to maintain the struggle for freedom and unity. Even if the PKK was destroyed as an organization, a society ready to stand up for its freedom and honor had been built, and a free people and individuals had been formed.

In conclusion, the Kurdish question was not resolved, but opportunities to solve it multiplied. Society anticipated a solution. Although the PKK was not able to sufficiently develop its solutions unilaterally, it was able to more strongly sustain its chance to resolve the issue. A nation-state solution is no longer its prerequisite, and it has paved the path to rich democratic political solutions. The state too is not able to impose its unilateral solutions. It is more aware than ever that it cannot continue to exist through such severe denial. A military solution has become such an expensive venture that the game is not worth the candle. Uncontrolled power often boomerangs on its owner. That is where we all stand. A dissolution and divergence similar to that experienced within the PKK has also taken place within the state. The state for the first time has had the courage to try itself under the name Ergenekon. The Republic of Turkey has for the first time in its history seriously entered the process of self-questioning. Numerous facts that have always been denied are now being expressed.

In this new era, the most important development is undoubtedly the meeting that took place between the President of the United States and the Prime Minister of the Republic of Turkey in 2007. Its contents have not been disclosed, but clearly they agreed to end Gladio's outdated methods in return for the cessation of the PKK's armed struggle. The Ergenekon trial is a concrete expression of this agreement. It was nearly a return to 1923; they were daring to correct an eighty-five-year-old mistake. The primary constituents of the Republic are coming together again. We are going through critical times again. Divided Kurds demand unity and integrity based on a renewed National Pact. History may go through many injustices, but it never forgets what happened. A time comes when the parties meet to overcome the injustices. No doubt the solution has not yet been reached, but we have entered the path to finding a solution. Hopes for the solution that has now appeared on the horizon become ever stronger every day. The Republic has the potential to create its own democratic model. We need to take the rich heritage of existing civilizations into account and be worthy of the spirit of unity that stems from a thousand-year-old fraternity and from being an ummah. If we do so, this potential will not only create its own model but will set an example for the unfortunate peoples of the whole region. The quest for a solution of the Kurdish question makes a democratic model not only possible but inevitable.

C — PROSPECTS FOR A SOLUTION IN THE KURDISH QUESTION

Capitalist modernity began to establish its hegemony in the Middle East at the beginning of the nineteenth century. Western hegemonic civilization, shaped by new factors and with a different center, brought to a new stage, indeed to the attention of history, social problems and solutions that had been unique to Antiquity and the Middle Ages. The Oriental question (which can also be defined as a general Middle East question) arose due to the disintegration of the Ottoman Empire. All societies, peoples, and nations have unique characteristics as well as common ones. The Arabs, Persians, Turks, Kurds, Armenians, Greeks, Assyrians, and Jews all experienced ever more problems based both on their nationality and religious denominations, such as Islam, Christianity, Judaism, and secularity, as well as on class-based, social, economic, political, ideological, and military considerations. New content and format were added to old problems, and the region became or was turned into an area of continuous crisis, conflict, and war. Western civilization had a deep-rooted superiority, and as this supremacy strengthened all countries, nations and societies inevitably focused on Western ways to resolve their problems.

History does not generate problems alone; the time and location where an issue is experienced carry with them the prospect for solution. It is thus important to realistically define the main sources of a problem and its possible solutions and then implement these solutions in terms of time and location. Sufficient discussion and clarity are of vital importance. In their absence, efforts to enhance discussions and find solutions will end up in a muddle. In the last two hundred years, the hegemony of capitalist modernity imposed this muddle on the Middle East. No group in society or any individual was unaffected by the numerous different methods implemented, such as the general divide and rule and the development of total hegemony.

Among the various peoples who have been adversely affected, divided, and suffocated with problems, annihilation policies, and rebellions, the Kurdish people are at the top of the list. During Antiquity and the Middle Ages, the Kurds and their ancestors experienced similar problems as a people and as a country. But during capitalist modernity, in addition to oppression and exploitation, the very existence of the Kurds for the first time was seriously and systematically threatened. During this period cultural and physical genocides were often visited on the Kurds. Within this general framework, in parallel with the evolution of the Kurdish question, the prospects for a solution changed and transformed as well.

The changes and transformations can be analyzed under three main forms.

1. The National Annihilation Solution of Capitalist Modernity

This is the most extreme and violent way to resolve issues in the cities and colonies of the capitalist system. The three fundamental elements of capitalist modernity—nation-state, capitalism, and industrial monopolism—try to form a homogenized social model in all the national societies into which they penetrate. They often resort to policies of denial and annihilation. The policy will differ depending on the resistance encountered. If it wishes to eradicate a social entity and dissolve it within its elements, the intense violence it applies can reach the level of genocide. The targeted community can be sent into exile outside its homeland, to besieged areas where assimilation is accomplished much more easily.

Being exiled from villages and rural areas to cities is another form of violence. In concentration camps, prisons, and massacres, the intensity of the violence is much more concentrated. Fragmenting the homeland is another form of violence, allowing a people to be ruled more easily. Forced assimilation also is another. Unemployment, poor health, prohibitions, and forced labor are types of systematic violence continuously being employed. Nonetheless if the targeted community or society survives and if its elimination is absolutely necessary, then the cultural genocide is complemented by physical genocide.

All the above-mentioned forms of violence have at different times and places been implemented in Kurdistan, and against the Kurds in the Middle East, by elements of capitalist modernity, their monopolist rulers, and especially their nation-states. It is insufficient to attribute these practices to the despotic rule and nation-states of Turks, Persians, and Arabs. Without the presence and approval of capitalist hegemonic headquarters, none of the despotic rulers or nation-states have the strength to apply their nationalist and annihilative violence. If the system does not give its approval, then a state can't make such an attempt, and even if it tries, it cannot maintain it.

From the beginning of the nineteenth century to 1945, the British Empire was party to all the nationalist-annihilative military expeditions, massacres, and fragmentations and to the local nation-states' (Turkish, Iranian, and Arabic) unique colonialist practices in relation to Kurdistan and the Kurds. If it were not for Britain and other hegemonic powers, the status of Kurdistan and the Kurds could not have been devised or enforced for the last two hundred years. But of course this does not mean that all responsibility falls on the imperialist capitals; the local elements of capitalist modernity, acting on their own responsibility, acted much more mercilessly and with the intent to annihilate. The backward and fascist state capitalism, nation-statism, and industrialism pushed them into this situation. Their late encounter with capitalist modernity and their poorly developed culture often compelled them to employ policies of denial and annihilation. Because capitalism was implemented in the form of state monopolism, it plundered, expropriated, and exploited, even in the absence of waged labor, and totally based itself on profits. Thus it had to rule the way it did.

It made sure that the private sector which it supported employed the same method. Clearly, such a state and private sector cannot easily be enforced in the absence of annihilation and forced assimilation. The nation-state, as an entity, is the biggest capitalist boss. It is the most organized and concentrated form of capitalism. This definition is significant in understanding what is happening. The nation-state's "social engineering" homogenizes in the name of the dominant national ethnicity. This tool operates mercilessly until the sections made "other" are eliminated. All the Arabic, Turkish, and Persian nation-states built in Kurdistan had such a function.

Industrialism is another practice of national annihilation and monopoly. Its destruction of agricultural and rural society represents modernity's biggest decimation of society. Industrialism, based on water, coal, and nuclear energy, has led to the evacuation of thousands of settlement areas as well as the elimination of all their cultural wealth, pollution, toxics, radiation emissions, and severe climate changes. Thus it is a threat worse than genocide. The destruction and plunder of antiquities in Kurdistan, the inability of the Kurds to freely express their culture, the bans placed on cultural values, and the absence of educational freedom for Kurds all point to a cultural genocide as dangerous as physical genocide.

Such social violence, also called the military solution, is linked to positivist Darwinism. Positivist Darwinism bases its right to life on the survival of the fittest. The Kurds top the list of those societies that have been subjected to the oppression and annihilation by governments using military power made possible by capitalist modernity. The Armenians, Greeks, Assyrians, Bedouins, and Turkomans have been victims of similar solutions. The desire to create a homogeneous, dominant nation is catastrophic. Each homogeneous nation is the result of the destruction of thousands of cultural values. Resistance and rebellions to defend one's existence and to protect one's honor against the practices of capitalist modernity and nation-statism usually resulted in massacres due to an asymmetry of power. Each massacre was a phase of the military solution. The fragmentation of Kurdistan with the National Pact, after it was divided with the Treaty of Zuhab (1639), increased the scope of the catastrophe and resulted in more intense military solutions. For the past ninety years, each part of Kurdistan was used as a guinea pig to test out military solutions. The "rebellious and backward Kurds" image has been intentionally created to justify military expeditions to crush and annihilate them.

The fundamental social power behind the military solution is the middle-class bourgeoisie and bureaucracy, which were created by modernity, made possible through the denial of the Kurds. The growth of this bourgeoisie depends on the exploitation of the Kurds and their unilateral bloodshed. Kurdistan and the Kurds are considered the natural resource or raw material for this class. They are never valued as a subject and are always treated as an object. They are kept at a level of slavery worse than that of women. They do not oppose the Western hegemonic powers, who implement a comparatively more relaxed policy of exploitation, because of their devotion to independence and freedom. The powers are afraid that this raw material will be taken from their hands and will then have an opportunity for better government. Thus they fear that this could incite the Kurds against their own rule.

Since the 1920s, the four nation-states (Iran, Turkey, Syria, and Iraq) have participated in an implicit and secret alliance when it comes to Kurds and Kurdistan, in return for concessions given to and protected by the Western hegemonies. In order to steer these local nation-states in any direction they choose, the hegemonies played with Kurdistan and the Kurds. They pretended to give them their support, then abandoned them once their own goals were achieved. No other people and their homeland have been subjected to such military force and conspiracies. The Armenians, Greeks, and Assyrians have all been the victims of such applications of modernity. The collapse of the Iraqi nation-state in 2003 left the rulers of Syria, Iran, and Turkey in a great panic: they set aside all their conflicts and problems in order to renew their secret alliance against the Kurds. They even forgot the religious fraternity to which they clung for so long and rapidly developed alliances—alliances never invoked against any enemy other than Kurdistan and the Kurds.

The Kurds rebelled against this layered hegemony and alliances, but in the absence of advocates and allies, they were able to develop neither a nation-statist solution (like their contemporary counterparts) nor a democratic nation solution. The dissolution of the Iraqi nation-state has led some Kurdish forces to want a federal state—a nation-state solution—but such a state is not very secure. Its formation does not liberate the Kurds; rather, the hegemonic and colonial powers use it as a tool of control. Its state military power has not abandoned the traditional goals in Kurdistan and toward the Kurds, but it no longer possess its old strength. It has been well exposed, and so it rapidly loses its collaborationist basis. The nation-statist military power solution relied very much on this social section. But after more than thirty years of resistance, the masks of these traditional Kurdish collaborationists have completely fallen, and they have been exposed. This erosion among the Kurdish collaborators is a major reason why the military solution is losing its strength.

When U.S. hegemony was established in Iraq, the basis for the counterguerrilla methods of NATO's Gladio also deteriorated. The tension between the Republic of Turkey and the United States over the PKK and the Kurdistan Regional Government developed further with the 2007 Washington agreement. The two parties appear to have achieved a general consensus on social, economic, political, and cultural solutions instead of a militarily dominated one; in return, the PKK had to abandon the armed struggle. The Ergenekon trials are related to this agreement. It also affects normal relations with the Kurdistan Regional

Government. Thus, the policies of the Turkish nation-statist administration toward Kurdistan and Kurds had to change. The other two pillars of modernity—the troubled profit rates of capital and its industrial interests over the Iraqi economy—have also been quite influential. The Republic's new Kurdistan and Kurdish policy was no longer dominated by military considerations solution and began to shift toward openness to compromise in economic, social, political, and cultural areas. No doubt this development is important; it will bear important results for all Kurdistan and for all Kurds and thus for the Middle East.

2. Kurdish Federalist Nation-State Solution

This solution is based on South Kurdistan and the Kurds who live there and essentially reflects the solution considered by the Western hegemonic powers. These powers are not so certain about the long-term success of local fascist nation-statist solutions, and they also feel that such a solution is not really suitable for their agreements in the region. Therefore the federalist nation-statist solution is an absolute necessity. Such a solution, based on the Southern Kurds, would be the best leverage for them to effect agreements in the related country and to enthrall and develop the local nation-states as well as the elements of modernity. Hence a fully independent Kurdish nation-state is unsuitable, since it could not provide the required leverage role. The Kurdish capitalist modernity started transformation toward the federalist solution both because their traditional collaborationist policies had been well exposed and because they no longer met even their own interests. The Kurdish federal state in northern Iraq (South Kurdistan) should not only be seen as the transformation of the bourgeoisie in the district but as the bourgeois transformation of the collaborationist class throughout Kurdistan. Its origins are deep-rooted. In all rebellions and nationalist organizations, such a solution has always been an objective. Despite being severely fragmented and dispersed, these forces can be defined as the Kurdish capitalist modernity.

The last thirty years of resistance, especially by the PKK, have forced the Kurds to achieve solidarity among themselves and to search for federalist solutions. They will insist on Kurdish nation-statism, although they may be scattered and disunited and subject to ideological and political weaknesses. No matter how much the local neighboring nation-states (Turkish, Iranian, Syrian, and even Iraqi central nation-state) oppose it, their existence will probably become permanent with the support of global capitalism. The global hegemony will find this model more suitable to its interests, and it will wish to implement it all over the Middle East. The fate of the federalist solution depends on the correct understanding of the Kurdish identity by the dominant nation-state's bourgeoisie and bureaucracy and the respect shown for this identity. Events in Iraq show that it has not yet reached this level. The Syrian nation-state considers the Kurds outside state society. It does not accept them as citizens. In Iran, the strict Shi'a nationalism is alien to the Kurds and is not suitable for their assimilation. It will take time to base the traditional state government on model elements. The present governance is far removed from federalism. The Turkish middle-class bourgeoisie and bureaucracy may rid itself of denial and assimilation much sooner. The intense cooperation between the majority of the Kurdish people and the Turkish upper class during the republic and pre-republic state formations may lead to a revolution of the mindset.

Besides, their strategic partnership during the establishment of the Republic is easy to remember. As the common history becomes correctly understood, acceptance of the Kurds within the state structures becomes inevitable. The Turks as a nation have experienced more than once that to be without the Kurds during critical times is a strategic disaster. During normal times too, albeit not federalist, it will be easy try to find new commonalities. The advanced intertwined lifestyles within a society may stimulate the wish for a common life. Since the left- and right-wing interpretations of nationalist ideology are already discredited and if the deep historical roots of ummah and nation are used in favor of conservative democracy, then the traditional Kurdish collaborationists will prefer to side with this. This is what is happening at the moment. Although the military solution is always kept as an option, it is possible to discuss federalism at least within the concept of freedom of thought.

Both the military solution and the federalist collaborationist solution have a narrow social capacity. Neither is in the interests of the Kurds or the neighboring communities. These models reflect the compromises reached among the upper-class elements of capitalist modernity. They will agree to the need for a solution, depending on how afraid they are of the lower social classes. The solution cherished by all national liberation movements and working-class unionism is that of the middle-class. The inability to resolve the existing problems is linked to this class structure. Each class has a certain solution capacity. To resolve the problems permanently, elements of democratic society not included in the capitalist modernity need to step in and play their historical roles. History does not offer sufficient conditions for the realization of Kurdish capitalist modernity.

The quest for a nation-state-based solution cannot surpass federalism. Federalism alone is an insufficient tool to resolve the Kurdish social question, which is in an acute crisis; it can, however, play a positive role within the democratic nation solution and thus compensate for its own shortcomings.

3. Democratic Nation Solution

The defining feature of democratic nation solution is that it seeks a solution outside the state. That means neither the construction of a new state upon the detritus of the old, nor becoming an extension of the present state and dissolving within it. Society searches for a solution within itself, within its democratic willpower. It targets the state neither positively nor negatively. Besides, throughout the history of civilization as well as during the era of capitalist modernity, the upper classes have always linked the solution to social problems and class interests to the establishment of a state. The demos has no possibility for such a solution. The proletariat or people's state solution proposed by real socialism on behalf of the workers and peoples is nothing but a deception and a delusion. Wars in the name of power and state have always been in the interests of the elite and capital. If democratic nation solutions were not implemented throughout the history, it is because they have not been in the interests of the elite forces and capital monopolies. The same is true for the attempts to resolve present-day problems.

The real reason for the deadlock was that the PKK, under the influence of real socialism, was for a long time unable to transcend the nation-statist paradigm. The situation is reminiscent of the way capitalist modernity has deadlocked the development of the Republic of Turkey. The PKK's aim was to transform the Republic of Turkey into a socialist state, establish a socialist republic in Kurdistan, and then establish an internationalist unity between the two of them. This paradigm leaves little room for democracy and democratic society. It did not grasp the class conflict inherent in power and state. Just as Karl Marx believed that a pure communist society could be established, it was believed that a pure class state could be formed. But of course phenomenally neither a pure class state nor a pure capitalist society is possible. Although the anarchists had some valid and correct criticisms, they were unable to develop the goal of a democratic nation society.

The PKK's democratic nation society idea has gone through a painful process of development. It is a rebirth, a rejection of the classical real-socialist party. It is a renunciation of the goal of the establishment of a state. Other political parties are going through a similar transformation.

The proposed democratic nation solution is not unique to Kurdistan and the Kurdish people. It is presented as a universal solution for Middle Eastern societies and everyone else. The political root of the democratic nation solution is the democratic confederalism of civil society, which is not state. Democratic confederalism is not the same as the state federalism or confederalism. They are different phenomena.

The economic-social model of the democratic nation solution is the communal unit. Ecological, social, and economic social units do not aim to make profit; determining and servicing fundamental needs is essential. The market may still exist, but monopoly over it is to be restricted and placed under the ethical control of society. The ethical and political values of society are to be placed above the law. Instead of the rule of law, priority is given to the principles of an ethical and political society. Criteria of direct democracy apply in the resolution of social affairs and problems, and direct democracy is proportional to the era's scientific consciousness. Freedom of society and the individual exists only when scientific consciousness, arts, ethics, and politics are intertwined. The level of freedom of the individual is linked to the level of freedom of the communal units he/she participates in. Detachment from society cannot mean freedom.

We can thus once again list the fundamental principles of the democratic nation solution alongside these general features.

a) Democratic Nation: This is a nation form of democratic society based on free and equal individuals with a multiethnic, multilingual system, with no room for class distinctions and state privileges. A democratic nation consists of the democratic citizen and communities. A flexible nation paradigm consisting of open cultural identities is essential.

b) Common (Democratic) Homeland: This is the sum of homelands that are equally and freely shared and where no individual or community is made to be "other" by another individual or community.

c) Democratic Republic: This means accessibility to the state for society and the individual. The state organizing itself and the democratic organization of the individual are two different phenomena and must be based on respect for each other's legitimacy.

d) Democratic Constitution: This is a constitution that is formed through social consensus, and protection of the democratic individual and communities against the nation-state is essential.

e) Inseparability of Individual and Collective Rights: Society is made up of individuals but is more than just their sum. Despite differences, individual and collective rights denote two different features of the same society. Just as there are two sides to a coin, the society or the individual cannot have either individual or collective rights; they must have both.

f) Ideological Independence and Freedom: The democratic nation solution cannot be accomplished unless the positivist ideological hegemony of democratic modernity and individualism—its reconstructed liberalist slavery—is overcome. Self-consciousness about its own social nature is the consciousness requirement of the democratic nation solution.

g) Historicity and the Present: Social realities are historical realities. The realities that occurred in history recur in the present with little variation. If we do not establish the correct links between history and the present, we cannot overcome capitalist modernity's individualism. This individualism has become drained of history as well as its social mentality. The correct understanding of history and the present is a necessary requirement for the democratic nation solution.

h) Morality and Conscience: Without referring to morality and conscience, no social problem can be soundly resolved. The solutions of modernity based solely on power and law yields no other result than to suppress and distort problems. In the democratic nation solution, empathy based on morals and conscience is imperative.

i) The Self-Defense of Democracies: There are no beings without self-defense, and thus this is also true for democratic societies; they are the most advanced beings of nature. They too cannot realize themselves or subsist without self-defense. The requirements of self-defense must be met within democratic nation solutions.

These frames of reference can be improved on, but they allow us to understand the democratic nation solution. They are the best cure for the social problems of the Middle East and especially for the Kurdish social problem. The democratic solution to be advanced in Kurdistan based on these principles and on the definition of democratic national life is of historical importance.

To have Turkey enter the democratization process and to have a democratic solution to the Kurdish question are two sides of the same coin. One cannot exist without the other. It may be clearer if we try to embody some aspects of the solution in the case of Turkey. Above all, the framework of references mentioned above cannot be ignored. Solutions without principles or systems are incomprehensible and can be only a temporary treatment. The envisaged solution, regardless of whether the Western capitalist hegemonic system survives or not, is to be cherished and implemented throughout this structural period.

First issue: The solution proposed is not just for the period of existence of Western civilization but has the potential to transcend it.

Second issue: No matter what the structure, institution and ideological monopoly behind the elements of capitalist modernity are, they recognize the existence of the democratic nation society and thus the legitimacy and existence of a solution. The democratic solution envisaged here does not propose the elimination of the elements of capitalist modernity (nation-statism, capitalism and industrialism) through revolution; nor does it accept the annihilation and assimilation of these elements through military means. It proposes that two fundamental entities that recognize each other's legitimacy coexist peacefully and enjoy a no-conflict competition.

Third issue: Democratic political institutions are indispensable to the first two issues. Democratic politics is the solution for all problems that may surface as well as for existing problems. Negotiations and diplomacy are included in democratic politics. All obstacles must be removed so that democratic politics can function. The existence of comprehensive freedom of thought, a democratically structured party, unions, cooperatives and all different types of civil society is only possible if present obstacles are overcome. Democratic politics must either drastically lower election thresholds or completely remove them.

Fourth issue: We need systems that can protect the right to self-defense of the main entities.

I attempted to define all these issues much more comprehensively above. Here I am trying to present them as implementable models.

4. The Name of the Democratic Solution: KCK

It is possible to make the democratic solution more concrete and even name it. It accepts the institutions and present borders of the Republic of Turkey as legitimate. There are no proposals for it to have a unitary, federal, or confederate character. What is proposed is that the democratic, equal and free aspects of Republic of Turkey's citizenship be not just defined in the constitution and regulations but institutionally implemented. To this end, the inseparability of individual rights and freedoms from those of collective, open cultural identities is proposed. It is also proposed that the issues related to the resolution of the Kurdish question are handled as an inseparable part of democratization, even as the basis for democratization. The solution is not state-oriented—it is based on a democratic system that includes the whole society. There is no need to repeat the fundamental issues of a democratic system as I have already comprehensively evaluated them. But it is possible to determine its name as the Union of Communities in Kurdistan (KCK). As has been frequently emphasized, the KCK should not be seen as like the Republic of Turkey or as its alternative. In both content and form, they are different formations. I have tried to evaluate the Republic of Turkey with its principles and institutions as well as its past and present and have no need to repeat it. But there is a requirement to define the KCK and to improve it. It is the umbrella organization constituted by the Kurds' democratic modernity elements (the democratic nation composed of economic and ecological communities, democratic compatriots, and open cultural identities).

The critical concepts here are democratic compatriot and nation. We don't need to discuss what a democratic compatriot is—such a person can be defined as one who has individual and collective rights and freedoms. Democratic nation may be a little more complex, but the European Union's definition of nation, deduced from the last five hundred years of modernity's bloody nationhood wars, is close to it. State nationalism is rapidly becoming flexible due to the congestion and problems it has caused. The emphasis is always on the democratic character of the concept of the nation. We could reconsider Mustafa Kemal's definition of "the People of Turkey are called the Turkish Nation." The extreme chauvinistic, male-dominated, and power-based contents given to the concept of Turkish nation makes its usage difficult. It impedes the participation of other identities. Thus "the People of Turkey" is quite close to my own proposal for the definition of a nation, one made up of open cultural identities and free and equal compatriots. Even in Mustafa Kemal's time, this concept denoted multiethnicity. Fanatical defense of a concept that has become an obstacle does not contribute to the solution.

For the Kurds, the KCK can be defined as the democratization of civil society. As the umbrella organization of civil society, it fits in perfectly with "the People of Turkey" or "the Nation of Turkey" and shares its essence. Indeed, if it is truly accepted that the Kurds should take their place within the People or Nation of Turkey, then this is clearly the most suitable and flexible definition. Only such a flexible definition of nation can prevent the problems generated by annihilation, denial, and federation. It is this flexible nation and umbrella organization, too, that can halt separatism and violence over the long term. Military force and federalist solutions do not have the capacity to resolve problems. On the contrary, historical and present-day experiences have shown that they continuously breed warfare and separatism.

Due to their present situation, the Kurds' communal nature has improved, and as individuals they have a very strong sense of emancipation. But pressing them to accept something less than this KCK solution would lead to a worse violence and separatism. At the very least it would allow them to accomplish their goals more quickly, as the existence of the Kurdistan Regional Government in Northern Iraq suggests. We remember the annihilation and denial policies throughout the history of the Republic. The knowledge we have gained through the social sciences assures us that the KCK solution would the most suitable for achieving a democratic Turkey, a democratic republic, and a democratic nation, and would have the highest probability of achieving these goals.

If the KCK solution is put into practice, the Republican institutions will of course continue in a new situation. While the state enforces itself administratively, the KCK will function as a set of democratic institutions. Both deal with issues. When a difference arises between them, more often than not they will complement each other. When there are similarities, a positive competition may commence, and the one that resolves problems the best will get the support.

The most important issue in this model is that neither should reject the other. All the traditional solutions, either state-centered or those with individual rights, are built upon rejection or "otherization." This mindset allows for no solutions that don't destroy or "other" them.

Religious and positivist dogmatism both contributed decisively to problems for society—and it still does. New data from social sciences emphasize that flexibility produces an advanced level of mindset in our social nature. Symbiotic relationships are prevalent, and antagonistic contradiction is unnecessary. Democratic political institutions (for which KCK should be seen as the umbrella organization) need not have a destructive relationship with the state. On the contrary, it pushes the state to become the most productive and necessary. Although there will be periods of tension, the extensive dialogue between them will make democratic solutions possible. If the process makes headway, then those institutions that are most necessary and beneficial will remain and develop, while those that are neither necessary nor beneficial will fall by the wayside. Indeed, such an outcome is to be expected from democratic mechanisms.

5. Possible Implementation Aspects of the KCK Solution

As we map out the implementation of the KCK solution, we must clarify several aspects.

a) Economic Aspect

The KCK will be in a position to defend society and the environment against the devastating effects of capitalist modernity, with its sole aim at achieving maximum profits. It will do so through economic and ecological communes, as well as other units aimed not at achieving profits but at responding to the fundamental needs of the society and protecting the environment. The social market will prevent monopolist profiteering. Capitalist elements will not be eradicated but will be strictly confined. Work will no longer be a chore but will express the joy of living. The walls of alienation built between life and work will be brought down. Instead of a system that commodifies everything in society and that overwhelms society with commodities, we will have an economic system based on use value and necessary exchange value. The ecological and social basis of the KCK is cut out for such a system. It will find solutions to social problems through the moral awareness that freedom is achieved by working—at the same time that it abolishes unemployment.

b) Social Aspect

The KCK system will respond to social needs in education, health, sporting activities, arts, and law. In these areas it will have a symbiotic relationship with the state as well as a competition. State institutions have not been able to deliver on expectations—the KCK will prove itself by functioning well. Contrary to widespread belief, language and ethnicity will not be much of a problem. Multilingualism in education is a social necessity and should be encouraged. Turkish, Kurdish, and other languages should all be taught, in order to enhance cultural richness. There is no need for either chauvinism or force. Institutions for education, health, sports, and art for Kurds, as for other cultures, will be developed within the context of the democratic nation and will enrich national integrity. If "the People and Nation of Turkey" ensures the integrity of cultural richness, then many issues that are today considered "problems" or "red lines" will in turn be seen as nothing but dogmatic, conservative prejudices. No stance can be more empowering than voluntary national integrity.

c) Security Aspect

Security is the area where decisions and regulations will have to be made. The Kurds have always not only lacked freedom but faced an existential threat. They will require robust assurances and institutional solutions. The Republican army is to be deployed against external threats, but in relation to the Kurds, it will have to go through a radical transformation. The same is true for all other security institutions. Until these transformations are complete, the KCK will have to have its own defense forces. As long as the village guard system, the present day JITEM, and other paramilitary groups (including those involved with Ergenekon) continue to exist, KCK self-defense units will be indispensable for democratic life. The army may be deployed in Kurdistan only against an external threat. The army must stop seeing the Kurds as a threat and accept them as fundamental to the integral unity of the state and nation. There should be a concerted effort to address the memory of painful events in the Republic's history. KCK self-defense units may take any of several forms; their status may be temporary or permanent. They may be included in the army and other security units (although not like the Iraqi Kurds) for local security.

d) Diplomatic Aspect

The most important problem here is how the division of Kurdistan and Kurds in violation of Misak-ı Milli (the National Pact) is viewed and what solutions are proposed. Of course Turkomans, Armenians, and Assyrians must be included here, as their circumstances will profoundly influence both internal and external policies. The developments in Iraq and Armenia are self-explanatory. The developments in Syria are also of importance, and what happens in Iran concerns the whole world. One should not view the Treaty of Zuhab as a thing of the past. We are running short of time. All these issues compel us to find solutions that are suitable for the whole Middle East; the KCK is the perfect opportunity to generate such solutions. It proposes a system that resolves problems without differentiating between ethnicities and nations but that takes denominational, ethnic, and national differences into account.

The model envisaged does not abolish borders, pave the way for a military solution, or impose federalism. Rather, it takes into account different models tried around the world, including the European Union, but with its own uniqueness. The KCK may be expanded as an umbrella organization to include all Kurds, Armenians, Assyrians, and Turkomans within a Turkey that encompasses all cultural identities. It does not have to include the states. The states may develop a European Union-type of union among themselves. A flexible confederation may be proposed, especially for Turkey, Syria, and Iraq. This model can then expand throughout the Middle East. The KCK model is not the opposite of a union of states but a democratic confederalism; it is a parallel and complementary union of civil society, created because of pressing social needs. In the history of the Middle East, many problems have not been resolved through the diplomatic activities of the state alone. Significantly, just as much as it is creating state confederations, the European Union is also trying to develop confederations of civil society. The present need for a society that can go beyond the nation makes such a solidarity organization indispensable. In the Middle East, confederalism of the states and democratic confederalism of civil society have equal importance and necessity. They must be developed in tandem and complement each other.

We may talk of other aspects of the KCK as well, but the abovementioned are sufficient for clarity and for making proposals. Undoubtedly, each aspect has constitutional and legal problems, as well as much legislation to be drafted. Achieving this solution will require intensive dialogue with the state security units, so that they contribute. The work of the government and the Grand National Assembly of Turkey will be pivotal. Dialogue and joint efforts that take place only on level of state institutions are insufficient; so are the efforts of the government and Grand National Assembly of Turkey taken alone. Civil society and opposition parties will also play an important contributing role. Public relations work is direly needed; the press and broadcasting organizations especially will play a vital role. The contributions to be made by universities and the academic world cannot be underestimated. The United States and the European Union are party to most aspects of the solution, and other international agencies with experience are expected to contribute.

These ideas for the democratic improvement of Turkey and the solution to the Kurdish question should be seen as proposals. I present this draft because I share responsibility. All concerned parties should now develop their own thoughts and proposals. As discussions and proposals develop, I will of course make further contributions.

What remains now is to develop an action plan to map out where to start and how to proceed. I present my proposal in the following section.

Part V: ACTION PLAN

If proposed solutions have no practical value, then they amount to mere brainstorming. The success of an analysis can only happen through practical action.

In my own case, I found that taking practical steps to resolve the Kurdish question, albeit amateurish, were more important than unilateral actions. Priority should always be given to meaningful dialogue. But I also know that self-deception in the name of dialogue brings disaster. One should not minimize the capacity of the parties involved for negotiation. The slightest ground for negotiation is more precious than the most advanced and successful physical action taken.

The PKK emerged in the 1970s, when a very strict denial policy in respect of the Kurds was in place. Even verbal opposition to this policy met with the most severe punishment. Back then I gave priority to joint democratic solutions with left-wing groups, as when I was elected to the presidency of the Ankara Democratic Association of Advanced Education (ADYÖD) in 1975. When this did not work, then it was inevitable that we would focus on the founding of the PKK. The initiative of August 15, 1984, was the only alternative against the policy of denial and annihilation. Although it was not as I had envisaged it, I did the best I could.

If the dialogue initiated in the early 1990s by President Turgut Özal had been furthered, the Kurdish question would be at a totally different stage today. The state did not give its own president the opportunity to engage in dialogue and negotiations; the traditional policy of denial and annihilation was in total operation. It was one of the darkest periods of the Republic's history. The attempt at dialogue on the political and military fronts in 1997 and 1998 suffered the same fate. The internal and external obstructions—in short Gladio, which had power over all political and military structures—did not allow for even the simplest attempts at dialogue and negotiation. Despite all my efforts to treat the İmralı interrogation procedures as grounds for dialogue and negotiation, someone continually spoiled it. All my proposals were left unanswered. It was clear that they were planning to eliminate the movement entirely. Some regarded negotiation and dialogue as signifying the end of their own power. They had grown strong and had become state within a state, and these sections were the most dangerous and merciless of all in their desire for power. Despite all my warnings, there was death by the thousands and innumerable material loss. Personally, since the 1990s I chose to limit warfare. But when this did not attain any results, I had to issue a last warning that a total resistance by Kurds and Kurdistan, although undesirable, was inevitable if they were to "protect their existence and attain their freedom."

It is not as if there are no plans among the parties to the war. Action plans are demanded and worked on a lot. I know this quite well from my own experience. Unilateral action plans are implemented passionately. But action plans that bring parties together are difficult to develop. In the absence of mutual empathy, such plans cannot be made. I will now briefly present my views on the unilaterally developed and currently implemented action plans and then suggest a possible action plan for reconciliation.

I do not see myself as one of the parties to the implementation—my present incarceration and the conditions under which it is enforced will not allow it. The opinion I offer here aims to ensure that the parties get to know each other realistically and gives information on a possible joint action plan.

1. The Traditional Plan of Denial and Annihilation.

Although not as much as before, there are still plans developed and implemented to attain this solution. Some interest groups that came into existence as middle-class bourgeoisie and bureaucracy obtained their wealth from the state. Although they have been discredited and isolated both internally and externally, they enforce their annihilation plans through insidious and brutal methods. The Kurds, apart from their collaborationist sections, responded by staging the most comprehensive resistance in their history. The PKK, as the leadership of the resistance, has the capacity and the power to comprehensively implement action plans. It is in a position to make a transition from passive defense to active defense and to all-out resistance. In the period ahead, the PKK will likely make the transition to all-out defense in the case of serious bottlenecks in the democratic solution.

2. The Federalist and Nationalist Plan

The traditional colonial nation-states and global hegemonic powers are behind this kind of plan, being implemented by the Iraqi Kurdistan Regional Government. Although they all have different aims, they agree in supporting this plan because they wish to diminish the Kurds' revolutionary and democratic potential. The United States is the hegemonic power that most openly supports the Kurdistan Regional Government, which plays a strategic role in controlling Iraq, Syria, Iran, and Turkey. Since the Second World War, the Turkish, Iranian, and Syrian administrations have been supporting the "Small Kurdistan" plan in northern Iraq, in order to break down the resistance of their own Kurds and to rule out their own Kurdistans. When the Kurds wish to overcome the role designated to them, these forces raise their objections all at once.

Politics and plans based on divide and rule are being mostly executed by the "Small Kurdistan" project. Revolutionaries, radical democrats, and socialists are to be countered in this manner. A fundamental aim of the plan is to isolate the PKK. A comprehensive Gladio operation works to isolate and eliminate the PKK in return for a "Small Kurdistan." This plan has wide support in international diplomacy. The U.S., Turkish, and Iraqi administrations, who have included the Kurdistan Regional Government among themselves, agree on this plan and are trying to lure the PKK away from armed struggle. But the plan is not yet fully executed due to the differing interests of the parties—its implementation remains limited. It holds no hope because Kurdish society does not widely support it and because it serves the interest of only a narrow elite sector. It is exposed and isolated ever more each day.

The response of the PKK to this plan is to not surrender and to continue to resist. Many of our people who were undecided or were morally and ideologically weak ran away and took refuge with the holders of this plan. The holders wished to create a new collaborationist movement, but they were soon exposed and discredited. Kurdish nationalism is traditionally quite weak, so they didn't develop a consistent nation-state plan. Their fate has been, so to speak, to become corrupt and then be eliminated. They had pinned all their hopes on the collapse of the PKK's resistance. The various Turkish governments had also long hoped for help from Kurdish nationalism based on "Small Kurdistan." They tried to implement a plan similar to the one implemented against the Greeks and Armenians on the basis of "Small Kurdistan." The plan has become counterproductive because of the different conditions and the position of the PKK. The subsequent backlash has made the position of the PKK even stronger.

3. The Democratic Solution Plan

Since the first two plans have not given much hope and have been in all respects very expensive, the Republic of Turkey has inclined toward democratization projects. Contemporary developments support this trend. The urgings of the United States and European Union, and a similar tendency in the media, civil society, the general public, as well as all the Kurds, now increase the feasibility of democratic solution plans. Despite the resistance of the nationalist-fascist front, which is now a minority, the fundamental institutions of the state are also not opposed to democratic solution plans. They are in fact preparing the groundwork. All this increases the chances of implementing the solution plans.

In this new historical situation, a feasible action plan must pass through a few stages. If the fundamental institutions of the state and the government reach consensus over the main features of the democratic solution plan, and if the Kurdish side and democratic forces support it, then these could be possible implementation phases:

a) The First Phase

The PKK will declare a permanent no-action period. During this phase the parties should be careful not to allow themselves to be provoked and should tightly control their own forces. They must prepare the general public.

b) The Second Phase

A Truth and Reconciliation Commission should be established at the initiative of the government, and the Grand National Assembly of Turkey should approve it. This commission is to prepare proposals that could remove legal obstacles. The parties must reach the greatest degree of consent on the composition of the commission. In relation to the confessions and defenses it hears, the commission will propose amnesty to the Grand National Assembly of Turkey. When legal obstacles are removed, the PKK can withdraw its extralegal structures outside Turkey, under supervision of the United States, the European Union, the UN, the Iraqi Kurdistan Regional Government and the Republic of Turkey. In time the PKK can position its forces in different areas and countries. It is critical that the release of those detained and convicted of PKK activity and the withdrawal of PKK armed forces outside the borders be jointly planned. Here the principle "neither will be implemented without the other" must apply.

c) The Third Phase

As constitutional and legal steps to democratization are taken, there will be no reason to resort to arms. All those who have been in exile for many years, especially those in the PKK, those who have lost their citizenship, and those who are refugees, can begin to return home. As the activities of the KCK gain legal status, the PKK will have no further need to engage in any activities within Turkey. It will base its further existence on legal and democratic political, social, economic, and cultural activities.

When it comes to implementing this three-phased plan, my own position is of strategic importance. It has a limited chance of implementation without Öcalan. Therefore a reasonable solution for my situation needs to be found.

Possible proposals in respect of my position are as follows:

I. It is necessary that I be released on the basis of a defense presented by me to the Truth and Reconciliation Commission.

II. I must be enabled to prepare all circles linked to the Kurds, especially the PKK, for the democratic solution and to help them adjust to the requirements of the plan within a framework of freedom but in alliance with the United States, the European Union, the UN, the Kurdistan Regional Government and the Republic of Turkey as well as, if required, representatives of other countries and powers.

III. There should be support to meet various needs, including and especially that of residency[35].

---

35 The Turkish term used here, *ikamet*, is (probably intentionally) vague and can include

The Turkish public and most Kurds have already intensively discussed the democratic solution and plans for its implementation. I have presented draft thoughts and proposals expected of me. I am certain that, on the basis of others' thoughts and proposals, I will have to revise, change, and improve my own.

Now that I have prepared this road map, responsibility falls on the AKP government as well as the authorities from the Grand National Assembly of Turkey and the fundamental institutions of the state. If they reach a general consensus, then there will be a need to start directly with the first phase. If not—and this is not a threat—then both the PKK and the KCK will be forced to mount "all-out resistance to protect the existence and freedom of the Kurds"—although this would not be something that I desire. Therefore we need to implement our plan for the democratic solution to the Kurdish problem.

all forms of residency like prison, house arrest or ultimately freedom.

Part VI: CONCLUSION

If the young Republic of Turkey had opted for a democratic solution to the Kurdish question, then the course of history would surely have been different. The blinding projects of capitalist modernity required Kurds to meet the same end as the Armenians. The world situation and the Kurds' own ideological and organizational weaknesses encouraged those with such projects in mind—they were sure they could repeat the success they had had with the Armenians. The middle-class bourgeoisie and bureaucracy had been raised believing in the erasure of pre-Republic history. For them, the Kurds had long ago been buried in history and had ceased to exist. Today they could be nothing but objects or disruptive elements. An unrestricted policy of assimilation could be imposed on them; the physical elimination of the Armenians could be repeated with the Kurds through cultural elimination. This generation was nothing like past generations of Turkish leaders, who had developed strategic alliances with Kurdish leaders at all the critical moments of their history. The Republic supported this new generation. In building a career, denying the Kurds was the silent golden rule. By renouncing Kurdishness, one could access any rank or position. This was the route to find one's place in the monopolies of modernity.

This denial and cultural genocide was only weakly challenged until the emergence of the PKK, which was perceived as a shocking threat. It should not have emerged, but it had. The last quarter of a century—which can only be defined as "extraordinary" and "horrible"—has shown that the path taken was a crime against humanity and led to excessive material and moral losses as well as degeneration. There can be no triumph with this path. But the Republic was established on the basis of an alliance of democratic elements, of which the Kurds were founding members. The monopolist modernity project conducted by the state was determined to erase from the system the other allies—the socialists and the Islamic ummah. The quest for a homogeneous nation reached the level of frenzy.

Contrary to claims, the architect of this project was not Mustafa

Kemal but the Unionist cadres. Just as they had used Abdul Hamid, they tried to use Mustafa Kemal through similar tactics. For the sake of determining truth, we must see the responsibility of these Unionist cadres for this plan of cultural genocide against the Kurds for what it was. The continuing Kızılelma (Redapple) alliance of left- and right-wing nationalists is fascist in nature and developed during the founding of the Republic as the antithesis of democratic alliance. They used komitadj and subversive approaches as their main methods within the state. They found good patrons within the United States and prior to that within the British Empire. In the last sixty years they oppressed society mercilessly with the backing of NATO's Gladio. Although the Ergenekon trial is symbolic, it nevertheless delivered a serious blow to their chance to once again become a state within a state. This situation is reminiscent of the elimination of the Yeniçeri (Janissary corps) during the rule of Mahmud II. The Janissary (who were good for nothing but deposing sultans and hanging grand viziers) were eliminated brutally in 1826, to pave the way for the Tanzimat and Meşrutiyet periods.

The modern Unionist Janissaries are at least a hundred years old. Not only did they drag the Ottoman Empire into collapse, they rapidly transformed the Republic of Turkey, which had democratic legitimacy, into a despotic government. The left- and right-wing nationalists, under the protection of British and U.S. imperialism instead of the previous German imperialism, had the same mentality and structures. In the last ten years, under the name Ergenekon, they conducted warfare based on plots and provocations within the state. They were not victorious this time, because their main patron, the United States, pulled its support. Their appeal for support from China, Russia, and Iran was fruitless, as was their Eurasia game. Their mimicking of Kemalism was even worse. But then one must not underestimate the remnants of their mentality and bureaucracy or their political representatives. They may not be able to reconstruct their hegemony within the state, but they can provoke and annul Turkey's democratic advances. Their experience and strength may be enough to achieve it.

In the Middle East and Turkey, crises and problems can be overcome only through comprehensive democratic advances. In this respect, in terms of its mentality and structure, Turkey has a chance to be a model.

Similar conditions to those that led to the rise of the Republic are now present for the democratic transformation of the Republic. History has renewed itself, as have the Kurds. They now face playing the role they played during their historical Anatolian and Mesopotamian alliances. They are no longer the Kurds they were once. They are renewed, organized, and active. Those who scheme will also no doubt continue to do so, due to their internal backwardness and conservatism.

The global hegemonic power, the United States, knows that it cannot rely on NATO's Gladio. After the collapse of the Soviet bloc, Gladio lost its meaning. Despite the best efforts of various Turkish administrations, Gladio's presence in Turkey lasted until November 2007. The PKK had spent its last twenty-five years fighting the Turkish Gladio (which was operating under the auspices of NATO). The interests of the United States, Israel, and the European Union in the Middle East and Kurdistan came into conflict with Gladio's old ways. The Republic of Turkey's institutions and governments were now opposed to the old ways of Gladio and wanted to overcome them. The most significant external obstacle to Turkey's democratization has thus become weak. Those who plot coups no longer have the support they once received.

Still, remnants of their mindset, structures, and ambitions will always be there and could be used when needed. During the founding of the Republic, they were used to prevent its establishment; later these structures were used to prevent its development; and presently similar possibilities could derail efforts for democratization. History is a unique treasure from which to learn lessons; in a present that contains the opportunity for freedom, one should seek maximum benefit from it.

The KCK (an initiative of the PKK, which has completed its democratic transformation, and of the Kurds, who are renewed and are preparing for the advent of democratic civilization) is the most suitable mechanism for achieving an honorable peace and democratic politics and for avoiding war. That makes it a robust foundation for a Democratic Turkey. The historical alliance of Anatolia and Mesopotamia is painfully re-realizing itself as the alliance of Democratic Turkey and Free Kurdistan. A look back at history is enough to ensure that those internal and external nuisances are not given a chance. History is an infallible compass for those who understand it. It is a source of inspiration and strength for those who know how to work with society and people of a democratic and free country.

In the event that this road map is implemented, it will mean not only a more independent Turkey but also a path to democracy, equality, and freedom for all the peoples of the Middle East. Democratic modernity, advanced against capitalist modernity's occupation and colonialism of regional culture, will gain the opportunity and strength to transform into a system in alignment with its own history. History might, perhaps for the first time, cease being the history of occupation, colonialism, and invasion, and become the history of a democratic, equal and free society.

Abdullah Öcalan
August 15, 2009
İmralı

Publications by Abdullah Öcalan

Declaration on the Democratic Solution of the Kurdish Question
Mesopotamien Verlag 1999, ISBN 978-3931885182

Prison Writings I: The Roots of Civilisation
Pluto Press 2007, ISBN 978-0745326160

War and Peace in Kurdistan
International Initiative Edition 2008, ISBN 978-3-941012-46-2

Prison Writings II: The PKK and the Kurdish Question in the 21st Century
Transmedia Publishing 2011, ISBN 978-0956751409

Democratic Confederalism
International Initiative Edition 2011, ISBN 978-3-941012-47-9

Index

N

O

P

Q

R

S